Saint Gaspar Del Bufalo
Saint of the People

by
Don Raffaele Bernardo C.PP.S.
Missionary of the Most Precious Blood

Bernardo, Raffaele

  St. Gaspar, Saint of the People

Bibliography

  1. Gaspar Del Bufalo, Saint   2. Christian

ISBN 1 - 895370-00-0

Translated and Printed in Canada 1990

Year of Current Printing - first year shown
1990, 1991, 1992, 1993, 1994, 1995, 1996, 1997, 1998, 1999,
2000, 2001, 2002, 2003, 2004

Published by the I Team - 54 West Beaver Creek Road,
Richmond Hill Ontario, Canada L4B 1G5 Tel. (416) 731-1115

Why another life of St. Gaspar?

For thirty–five years Primavera Missionaria, a modest little newsletter, has been distributed to a large number of Italian families throughout the country.

Through this means St. Gaspar's fame has spread and he has become widely loved and venerated in our day, a multitude of the sick and needy come to him with faith and devotion. He answers their calls with loving largesse and intercession, so that the miracles obtained though grace are truly numerous. Anyone can verify this, whether by checking through the information published in the little newsletter or by visiting his Church in Albano Laziale, where the testimonials are collected in a large number of albums.

But do those who are devoted to him truly know St. Gaspar?

What do people know of his charisma and his life except for those episodes, the LITTLE FLOWERS, which Primavera Missionaria publishes?

Quite a number of books have been published on the life of St. Gaspar, especially recently. However, we don't think that they are all accessible to everyone since they were not produced for mass distribution.

The first biography of the then Blessed Gaspar was written in 1904, on the occasion of the beatification of the Servant of God, by Mons. Vincenzo Sardi. This remained the only work on his life until a truly attractive biography on him by the writer, Luisa Santandrea was published in 1943 and attracted great literary acclaim.

Once these two books were out of print, I published in 1949, right after the Second World War, a little booklet titled The Blessed Gaspar Del Bufalo. Several thousand copies were printed and were so well received. thus, the first well–illustrated biography of the Saint saw the light. In 1954, the year the Saint was canonized, G. De Libero's book, St. Gaspar Del Bufalo the Roman, rolled off the presses. In 1969, when devotion to the Saint was becoming widespread, we published a booklet by Don Gennaro Cespites, which contained many illustrations and which circulated widely. Several hundred thousand copies have been printed and it was still available until recently. (Editor's

Note: The English version of Don Gennaro's book was published in Toronto in 1984.)

However, the "life" which most knowledgeable people waited for was the one written by A. Rey. which had been in typed manuscript form since 1942 but given its size and strained financial circumstances, had never been published. This work appeared in 1979 in two richly illustrated volumes. This biography remains, to date, the most complete and well–documented available, even though its style is somewhat dated and, given the fact that the Institute Archives were somewhat in disarray at the time, the quotations and the attributions are not always accurate.

Before Rey's work was published, the biography of Prof. Giorgio Papasogli had appeared, but, for some reason, it did not have the success that was expected of it.

Among the more recent books on him are:

I Fioretti di S. Gaspare (1985) which I wrote. Rather than a true biography, it is a collection of episodes in the Saint's life. On the occasion of the Bicentennial of St. Gaspar's birth (1986), Don Beniamino Contini edited Gaspare Del Bufalo – One Saint Scrutinizes Another Saint. This book contains the sworn deposition of the Venerable Giovanni Merlini, given during the Trial for the beatification and canonization of the Venerable Don Gaspar Del Bufalo. It deals, then, with the most authentic and genuine information available on the life of the Saint. Don Beniamino also prepared for publication in the same year the Life of St. Gaspar in comic book form.

When the booklet by Cespites was no longer available, I was asked to publish yet one more "short biography" with colour illustrations and a more modern format. Thus was born Don Gaspar Del Bufalo, a Saint of the People. Obviously, I followed to some extent the format of my previous booklet and used the information available from my predecessors, in particular Merlini and Rey.

The intent of this book is to offer the devotees of the Saint a brief and readable biography in a simple style.

Why have I added the subtitle "Saint of the People"? Are not all Saints, Saints of the people? I think that in the life of St. Gaspar this aspect should be stressed more than in the lives of other Saints, because for Gaspar, the word people means all the people.

He was born of ordinary folk, even though his family had its roots in that of the Marquis Del Bufalo. Two commoners, Antonio Del Bufalo, assistant–cook and then cook to Prince Paluzzo Altieri, and the very devout Annunziata Quartieroni were his excellent parents. They lived in one of the most beautiful and sumptuous palaces in Rome, but the family occupied very modest quarters facing the inner courtyard. What is most significant, is that Gaspar was never touched by thoughts of having liveried servants and honours, he spent his childhood among the sons of servants and the children of the poor.

His first concern was for the poor and the children of the people; his first apostolate occurred among the "farmers", the shepherds and the unemployed looking for work in the Capital, in Campo Vaccino (the present–day Roman Forum). All of his apostolic life was spent among the people and on behalf of them. He was the Saint of the people not only because he loved them and defended them through numerous sacrifices, struggles and persecutions; but because he was much beloved by them.

Entire towns would rush to listen to him preach; the churches and convents were not large enough to hold the crowds; he had to give his sermons from a platform erected in the squares. He was always meticulous in seeing that all classes of society, whether on his Missions or in Rome, received his attention and his words of comfort.

In the squares, banners would be displayed with such messages as: "Don Gaspar, you have stolen our hearts". The sinners assailed his confessional; people blocked the roads to keep him from leaving town.

They loved him because he would courageously defend the poor, the persecuted and the oppressed. He would visit and care for the sick wherever he went, he would teach the children, receiving them along with the old and the homeless in the hospice of St. Galla. In particular, he took care of those suffering and the children thrown into the Correctional Prison. He visited and comforted those who were in prison, pleading the cause of those who were innocent. He saved the town of Sonnino from being demolished. Even though he was weak and ailing, *he rushed from Albano to Rome, in the middle of August, to alleviate the sufferings of those afflicted by cholera. He was loved by the people because he preferred to stay in the small towns, living among the simple inhabitants there, sharing their pain and their sorrow.*

We believe that there are few Saints who, like him, so loved the people and in turn were loved by them.

Even today St. Gaspar is the Saint of the People.

The little newsletter that speaks of him is requested and read all over Italy. There are many who, if they don't already receive it, phone to ask that it be sent to them. They say: "If we don't receive it, it's like being deprived of a dear friend and a protector of our family. We wait for it because St. Gaspar arrives along with it to comfort us and give us hope." Thousands of people, singly or in groups, come daily to pray in this simple church of his, this church which is so beautiful, secluded and, above all, so prayer–inspiring. We constantly see people crying and imploring him for his grace or thanking him with tears of gratitude. Even in Rome, in Crociferi Square and in all the churches where his image is displayed, the faithful arrive in large numbers. Thus does this Saint continue, even from Heaven, to remain among the people which he so loves, in order that they may be redeemed by the Blood of Jesus.

Don Raffaele Bernardo
Missionary of the Most Precious Blood

Albano Laziale 15/02/89

HIS BEGINNINGS

Gaspar as a child, in grave danger of losing his sight, is cured by the intercession of St. Francesco Xavier.

In the confessional of the monastery of the Visitation in Rome a humble and saintly nun, sister Maria Agnese of the Word Incarnate, inspired by God, said to her father confessor, Canon Francesco Albertini, later to become Bishop of Terracina:

"You will meet within the confines of the Church a young priest, inspired by the glory of God. With him you will form a close friendship and during periods of oppression from enemies and times of tribulation, you will be his director. He will distinguish himself by his special devotion to St. Francis Xavier. He will become an apostolic missionary and will found a new Congregation of missionary priests under the invocation of the Divine Blood whose purpose shall be to reform customs, to save souls, to foster decorum among the secular clergy, to arouse the people from their apathy and lack of faith, bringing them back to the love of the Crucifix. He will found an Institute of Nuns which, will not, however, enjoy his leadership. Finally, he shall be the Herald of the Divine Blood and rouse sinners and sectarians alike during Christianity's times of trouble."

Mons. Albertini was overcome by a wave of joy upon hearing that, sent by God, the Apostle of the Blood of Christ would come. He himself had founded the Archconfraternity of the Precious Blood in the basilica of St. Nicola in Carcere in Rome, where a famous Relic of the Blood of Christ was venerated.

The man chosen by God was born in Rome, in a hovel on the Esquiline Hill, on January 6, 1786, the son of Antonio Del Bufalo and Annunziata Quartieroni, both good Christians, charitable and "di civil condizioni". He was so fragile and delicate that it was feared he might not survive. He was thus baptised the very next day in the basilica of Saints Sylvester and Martin of the Mountains and given the names of the Magi: Gaspar, Melchior and Baldassar. Henceforth he was always called Gaspar.

His genealogical tree reveals Gaspar to be a descendant of the noble family of the Marquis Del Bufalo, a title which he always refused to acknowledge, saying: "I am the son of a servant." Once when they called him "Marquis", he answered firmly: "I am Canon Gaspar Del Bufalo."

From the hovel on the Esquiline Hill, Gaspar's family moved to the ground floor of Palazzo Altieri, which stands beside the famous Church of Jesus when his father, Antonio, was taken on as an assistant cook by the Prince. Gaspar was to remain here until he went to prison.

One particular episode reveals how dear he was to God. At the very tender age of eighteen months he suffered such a violent bout of smallpox that the secretions from the pustules flowed into his eyes and threatened to leave him totally blind. His mother, after trying every remedy at her disposal, turned, as is often done in desperate situations, for help to St. Francis Xavier, the marvellous Apostle of the Indies whose arm was venerated in the Church of Jesus . The cure was immediate and total. Gaspar was never to forget St. Francis Xavier and one day he would choose him as the Patron of his Congregation, thereby raising a perpetual altar to him in his heart and in the hearts of his numerous brothers and all the souls whom he and his fellow missionaries converted.

Once cured, the boy immediately began his miraculous rise. If, from the restless character of his father he inherited the enterprising spirit for the glory of God, it was from his mother that he received his solid piety, his ardour in prayers, his refined taste and manners, his studiousness, and his generosity towards the poor, which was such that he was to deprive himself of breakfast and part of his lunch and dinner in order to give them to those who came to knock at the bars of his cell. From both his parents he inherited the firmness of faith and the dedication to the Church which, as we shall see, would lead him to perform so many acts of heroism.

THE ROME OF ST. GASPAR

The effects of the French Revolution had been felt from one end of the peninsula to the other. The first revolutionary movements of the patriots who aspired to the Unification of Italy took place in Lombardy and from there spread to the other States, particularly to the Republic of Naples. The new ideas had also gained ground in the Papal State, giving rise to numerous Masonic Lodges and various other Sects, all of which were motivated by deep anticlerical feelings. The alliance of the Freemasons and the Carbonari coupled with anticlerical sentiments would increasingly form the basis on which the future patriotic movements would be founded.

The Rome of that era was, clearly, very different from the Rome of today; but even then it was a city of marvels, the place that all of Christendom dreamt of visiting. To the monumental remains of the Ancient Roman Empire had been added the opulence of the works created by the genius of the greatest architects, sculptures and painters in the world. Their art had enriched not only the city itself, but also the sumptuous villas of the Roman patricians dotting the surrounding area known as the Castelli Romani.

The people of Rome, although pre–eminent in their faith and in their profound fealty to the Pope, took every opportunity to express their innate cunning and their pleasure–loving nature, which was given vent in the famous pasquinades and in the renowned Roman Carnival. "The Roman populace does not overly exert itself when working; they love to eat well and enjoy themselves."

But this was not the Rome of which Gaspar was proud and he made a point of identifying himself as a true "Roman from Rome". For him Rome was the beacon of light for the people of the world, the city of Christian thought, the centre from which Grace and the Word radiated outward, the city which united everyone and made all men brothers.

He saw in the imposing monuments which surrounded him not the greatness of the Rome of the Caesars, but rather the places which had soaked up the blood of Peter and Paul, and so many other Christian martyrs. It was certainly not in Gaspar to look longingly at the haughty magnificence of the great palaces

and the princely villas. He did live in the palace of a prince for a time, but he occupied the most modest room there, untouched by the richness which surrounded him. He was to remain modest in everything, in spirit as well as in the life he led. He loved the narrow side streets, the tiny unkempt houses with the threadbare clothing hanging out the windows to dry dripping on the passers–by. Gaspar's heart ached at the scores of dirty and ill–clad children he saw all about and the bearded vagabonds who spent the night in the open. The sight of so much misery tempered his soul, and as he matured, the soul of an apostle began to form in him.

At the age of eleven he enjoyed all of the heavenly sweetness of First Communion. He had prepared long and hard for it and through meditation he received the decisive call to his vocation and gave himself entirely to God. Guided by men of indisputable spiritual stature, such as Don Eugenio Pechi, Abbot of the Monastery of the Holy Cross in Jerusalem, and Abbot Giovanni Marchetti, he made enormous strides on his journey toward God. He became active in the Church of Jesus and avidly attended all the lectures given there by the great orators and the teachers of asceticism and moral theology. He was overcome almost to the point of delirium by a desire to experience pain and to do penance "in order to make his suffering one with that of Christ". His mother discovered, to her horror, blood stains on his sheets and he blithely confessed that he wore a belt of sharpened iron points to bed "in order to expiate his own sins and for the conversion of sinners".

He stopped wearing it when his confessor told him it was a sin to do such penance without permission. His childhood friends: Maria Tamini, daughter of the steward of Prince Altieri, later to become a nun, followed Gaspar with her prayers and counsel her entire life; Filippo Brera, later to become a Basilian monk; Carlo Valletta, who became a cardinal, and others listened with compunction to the sermons of the young Gaspar who scourged himself as he preached in his own house from a

Gaspar, the little apostle, amongst the barozzari of Campo Vaccino (Roman Forum)

chair which served as his "pulpit".

They never questioned his orders, even when he put together a plan to run away and preach the faith to...the Turks.

THE STUDENT

When Gaspar turned six, his father, Antonio, despite his poverty, saw to it that his son received an education and entrusted him to the charge of a teacher named Vizzi. The latter came to the house and taught the boy the rudiments of reading and writing. At the age of seven he was sent to the Scolopi Fathers where he studied assiduously and learned a great deal.

As his mind filled with the knowledge he received, his spirit grew ever more rapidly. The traits we find reported in the various biographies of the young Gaspar of this period are not very flattering; he is described as vain, impetuous, almost aggressive, irascible, punctilious, quick to snap... From this we can see what an effort, aided by Grace, he had to make to control himself. When he felt himself on the verge of anger or of rebelliousness, he would screw up his face and say: "I won't get angry, but if only you knew what's going on inside me!" And he would conclude: "Heavenly Mother, help me!" His own mother, ever meek and mild, was so helpful with her words of affection and her own example, that the boy gained full mastery of his own personality and became so accomplished and kind that he acquired a reputation as a perfect gentleman. He would be diligent at mass, serving those old meticulous priests, whom everyone tried to avoid because of their longwindedness.

At the age of ten he received permission to wear a cassock and he was fully aware of the significance that such a privilege entailed. He was very concerned that it should always be kept clean and his mother, ever proud of her son's achievement, used to say with a smile on her face: "With this son of mine, I'm always busy with the clothes brush."

His demeanour and his modesty attracted everyone's attention. Some said he was another St. Louis, but, generally he was known as the Little Saint. One day Prince Don Paluzzo Altieri saw him in the palace courtyard and was so taken by Gaspar's behaviour that he said: "Here is our Little Saint," and doffed his hat in deference to him. The Princess added: "Remember us to God in your prayers!" "Your Excellency, it is my duty to do so," Gaspar replied, somewhat flustered. By this time Gaspar was ready to move on to the College of Rome.

For three centuries this famous school had been a centre of knowledge and piety, the alma mater of a host of saints and learned men. Now it totally absorbed our Little Saint and tested his intellectual powers to the limit. He completed all his studies there: rhetoric, philosophy, dogmatic and moral theology, sacred scripture, ecclesiastical history and Hebrew. He also took private lessons in the art of preaching. As his marks testify, he was a model student.

He worked very hard, spending hour after hour at his desk in order to master, not only the required subjects, but other disciplines as well. In later years, he was to repeat over and over again to his fellow brothers that a Missionary must be not only saintly, but learned.

The horizon of his yearning for holiness and goodness and his desire to serve his fellow man quickly widened. The world surrounding Gualtieri Palace and the College of Rome was becoming too narrow for the apostolic zeal of young Gaspar and he looked further afield. He came to know the material and spiritual poverty afflicting Rome and was incapable of remaining apathetic and indolent. He wanted to help everyone and comfort them with words of hope.

THE YOUNG APOSTLE

So vast and so varied was the apostolic work of his youth that it would take too long to speak of it here in detail. Suffice it to say that there was no corner of Rome which remained untouched by his influence.

We must keep in mind two key dates in the life of the Saint: April 12, 1800, the day he received his first tonsure* (the old rite of acceptance into the clerical state) and February 21, 1807, the day he became a Subdeacon and officially entered the clergy.

* *tonsure – the shaving of the head or a portion of the head upon admission to the priesthood or to some monastic order.*

He would consider these events to be a genuine covenant with
God: he would dedicate himself entirely to His service and to
the salvation of souls.

Before Gaspar had received the holy orders, the old parish
priest of St. Mark, impressed by his abilities and achievements,
had already entrusted to him the teaching of Christian doctrine
to the young children of the parish. To those who were critical
of the priest's judgement he replied: "Go and listen to him and
you'll see that he's better at it than I am." The Barnabite Father
Antonio M. Cadolini, later a Cardinal, was so taken by Gaspar
after he heard him preaching that he said: "Keep your eyes on
him, he will be a great orator." One devout woman shouted at
him the words of the woman in the Gospel: "Blessed is the womb
that gave you life and the breast which gave you milk!"

The young man was not satisfied with being a student,
teaching catechism, preaching and performing works of charity
in the streets and at the hospitals. He also took part in all the
Roman institutions of prayer and in the instruction and education of abandoned children, initiating and promoting new activities in the field. At St. Alessio he instituted the nocturnal
adoration of the Most Holy Sacrament; at St. Pudenziana he
founded a society to which he gave a broader scope by allowing
the participation of young people who did not necessarily have
a calling for the ecclesiastic life. He approached the young,
encouraging and inspiring them, instructing them to the point
that this new work in Rome kindled great interest. Vain/glory?
Not at all. He was a born organizer, a man of vision. And his
purpose was to spread the knowledge and love of Christ in order
to alleviate the ills of humanity.

The list of institutions that he founded is endless, so we will
mention only a few at random. Union of St.Paul to teach the
poorest and help the most abject; the Confraternity of the Holy
Rosary and of Christian Doctrine in St. Mary of Sorrows.

The Pious Union of Mt. Carmel; the Perpetual Adoration at
the Pantheon; the Confraternity of the Red and the White
Sacconi; weekly preaching at St. Orsola; the Ecclesiastic Subsidy for the poor among the clergy; the Christian Doctrine in St.
Apollinare. The pearls of his zeal were his apostolate among the
barozzari (carters), the Work at St. Galla, the Hospital of the

"Cento Preti" and his work at the Correctional Prison.

The Mission Among the Barozzari (Hucksters) came about entirely through his own initiative and took on a truly new and unusual aspect under his tutelage. A host of farmers and hucksters from the surrounding Roman countryside had taken to bringing hay and other produce to Rome to sell it at a profit. Everything was stockpiled at Campo Vaccino, the ancient Roman Forum, which was thus reduced to a market place and pasture. To swell the ranks of these so–called hucksters or vendors, workers of all kinds came in droves from the surrounding regions of Marche, Abruzzo and Campania to work for mere pennies a day, so great were their misery and hunger. Swearing and vile language were the common means of communication. Because of the ever–present wine, there were constant brawls, and stabbings were not an uncommon occurrence. Gaspar asked himself: "How long has it been since these poor souls with calloused hands and parched by the sun have heard anyone talk to them of God?" In that open field Gaspar was to compose the most beautiful page of his preparation for the clergy. He was an aspiring little priest, a neat and tiny figure mingling amongst the masses of men and beasts, the butt of jokes and pranks. Unmoved, the young Gaspar began to approach a few of them. A word here and a small gift there, served to break the ice. Insults turned to curiosity, then to interest and finally to respect. They would hoist him up on a stack of hay and from there the little priest would recount the parables and stories from the gospels and speak to them of the love of God and of the Blood shed by Christ for them. Being a good teacher, he added to his sermons a touch of pathos: their youth, the memory of their First Communion, praying as they sat on a mother's knee, a mother who had white hair and perhaps had recently passed away, their brides, their young children... Here and there, on the hardened faces of the bearded men, a tear could be seen. Soon Gaspar was eagerly awaited every day. The Mission was consolidated with precise rules. They were to accept God and respect His law; they were to organize themselves in the spirit of friendship in order to find work at fair wages; they were to see that those in authority heard their concerns. It was, in essence, a trade union before its time. The Mission flourished but not without tears,

O. Scarpelli

calumny and many struggles for Gaspar. There were those whose interests lay elsewhere and who had other plans for exploiting the poverty of the hucksters and vendors.

One day Gaspar passed by the Hospital of St. Galla which had been rebuilt by Pope Gregory VII at the foot of the Rupe Tarpea where the Roman matron, Galla, had turned her palace into a refuge for the early Christians. In that Hospice many Roman priests, including Saint Giovanni Battista De Rossi and father Parisi, had outdone each other to alleviate the sufferings of the poor and sick of Rome. Seeing that it was so neglected and run down he said firmly, first to himself and then to others: "It must flourish again." Everyone said he was crazy and giving himself airs. Many famous people with great talent and the means had tried before him without succeeding. They didn't realize that love is oblivious to all limits and obstacles. He tracked down old benefactors and found new ones, he held out his hand, he knocked on doors, he began to improve and reinstate the acts of charity – everything was to have its source in God – education and aid. He would go into the squares, the shacks, the hovels and cry out: "Young and old, you who are in need, come, come to Santa Galla!" He went so far as to carry some of these dregs of humanity on his shoulders to the Hospice where they found cleanliness and comfort. A bowl of soup and Gaspar's love would warm their hearts while he cured their bodies and re-deemed their souls. All of Christian Rome benefitted and lent a hand to the courageous young man. As long as Gaspar lived, the Mission prospered.

His zeal also led him to the correctional home at St. Albina. The young inmates, accustomed to the whip, were fascinated by the young priest who spoke to them with such kind words. He even took them unescorted on walks through the city; they never betrayed him. And as adults, when they got out of prison, they knew to whom they could turn. Gaspar would write little plays for them, and today few realize that he was the founder of the first parochial theatre. He turned every means he could to advantage in order to help mould the character of the young.

Gaspar courageously refuses to swear allegiance to Napoleon.

The young priest also found the time to spend many hours in the Hospital of the "Cento Preti", where the clergy who were too old or too ill spent their remaining days. What a delightful scene: the young Gaspar, on the threshold of his own Ordination, caring with such affection for those who had come before him and who were now waiting to be called from this life.

We shall repeat here the words of De Libero: "Many people gave of their time and contributed to that immense spiritual richness of tradition, institutions, and charitable works of which the Rome of the nineteenth century was justifiably proud. It was to them that she owed her reputation as the capital of the Spirit and of Charity. But no one contributed more, first as a young man and then as a priest and Missionary, than Gaspar did." That is why John XXIII in addressing the young members of Catholic Action used Gaspar as an example, telling them that they could venerate him as the precursor of their own Movement.

A PRIEST OF GOD

On February 21, 1807 Gaspar had been ordained a subdeacon. On March 12, 1808 he was ordained a deacon and on July 30 of the same year he was elected Canon of the Basilica of St. Marco which is located behind the present day Palazzo Venezia. All that remained at this point was the decisive step, Ordination into the Clergy. However, reflecting on the dignity of the priesthood and the great responsibility that went with it he asked himself: "Will I be worthy of it?" The noble figure of St. Francis of Assisi flashed through his mind, for he had in his humility remained a deacon. The devil, already aware of all the souls the little priest would take away from him, tempted his soul and terrified him.

Gaspar was very humble and therefore knew not only that he was unworthy, but that he needed to seek the advice of others as well. He began to ask the advice of learned men and holy priests and he asked all the pious souls he met to pray for him. Do you remember Maria Tamini, the young girl who was his friend during their childhood? She was now a Sister of the The Pious Teachers. Well, Gaspar wrote to her also so that she might pray for him. Sister Maria did not spend much time reflecting and forwarded Gaspar's letter immediately to the holy bishop of Macerata and Tolentino, Mons. Vincenzo Maria Strambi, a Passionist, whom Gaspar knew well and held in great esteem. Mons. Strambi had no doubts and said to Sister Maria: "Write to Don Gaspar to proceed to the Altar and not to worry; his doubts are all the work of the devil."

Gaspar obeyed and on July 31, 1808 he was ordained a priest. On August 2 he celebrated his first mass in St. Marco where on July 30, 1808 he had already been made permanent Canon.

THE ROMAN STRONGHOLD

A tragic period was about to descend on the Church. In 1807 Napoleon had already threatened and insulted Pius VII by invading the Papal States. On February 2, 1808 an infantry unit of the French army commanded by General Miollis entered Rome and occupied Castel Sant'Angelo and Piazza del Quirinale where the Pontiff was staying. The Pope sent word to Napoleon that he considered himself a prisoner and had no intentions of negotiating with France.

Gaspar spent this period of general anxiety in increased prayer and redoubled his pastoral activities. Meanwhile on December 8, 1808 a very significant and decisive event in the life of our Saint occurred: the birth of the Archconfraternity of the Most Precious Blood in the church of St. Nicola in Carcere, in Montanara Square. Invited to preach a sermon for the occasion, he met for the first time Canon. Francesco Albertini, who became his spiritual father and was to become his companion and director during his imprisonment. Albertini immediately saw in him the preordained Founder of the Congregation of the Missionaries of the Most Precious Blood whom Sister Maria Agnese of the Word Incarnate had revealed to him.

In this basilica a piece of the mantle of a Roman soldier of the noble Savelli family was venerated. According to tradition, while he stood beneath the cross his mantle was stained by the Blood of Jesus. The stains were still visible on that piece of material, and for that reason it had been preserved with great care and veneration. Who besides Gaspar could have given the inaugural address? The plot so admirably woven in heaven, that

is, the plan to bring together these two great souls, was miraculously unfolding as it should.

Napoleon had the Cardinals arrested, despoiled Rome of her countless works of art and riches, had the papal coat of arms taken down and on May 17, 1809, he proclaimed an end to the temporal power of the Pope. The Pope's response was immediate; he had the papal Bull of excommunication posted in all the basilicas of Rome. In retaliation for this, the Pope himself was taken prisoner and deported to France and the bishops and other dignitaries who had remained faithful to the him were deposed. An Napoleonic decree ordered all priests to swear allegiance to the Emperor on pain of exile and imprisonment if they refused.

Gaspar too, on the morning of June 13, 1810 received a summons to appear at the police station. His father wanted to be with him at all costs.

The police official's name was Olivetti, so we know that he was a renegade.

On being asked to swear allegiance to Napoleon, Gaspar's answer was swift and clear: "I cannot, I must not, I will not." So much courage aroused not only anger, but also admiration. They tried to persuade him first with promises, then with threats; but his answer did not vary. They then tried to get his father to reason with him. "Citizen, have me shot first and then my son, but don't speak to me of swearing allegiance." Antonio, despite his faults, was as indomitable as his son in his love of the Church and its Leader. Gaspar was sentenced to exile and imprisonment.

Here the reader may be moved to ask: "Why did Gaspar defend the temporal power of the Popes?" At that time the question did not arise and the temporal power of the Pope was never questioned. Neither Gaspar nor his father considered this to be an issue. They were Romans and Napoleon was an arrogant foreigner who had come to occupy the sacred soil of their homeland; the Pope was virtually an unarmed sovereign who had never engaged in warfare to defend his temporal power.

Gaspar comforts his fellow priests in prison, exhorting them to suffer for Christ

Napoleon, on the other hand, had come with arms and arrogance to drag him away as a prisoner. Napoleon's soldiers were causing havoc in Rome, pillaging, sacking and despoiling churches and museums all over Italy. The General had even imposed a new catechism. Even Mazzini, who certainly couldn't be accused of "religious sympathies" was later to comment on the situation by saying that Napoleon acted only out of a desire to lay down the law for the whole world.

When he got home, Gaspar burst into tears. He must immediately leave behind his adored mother, his father, his friends and colleagues. He must forthwith depart from his beloved Rome and abandon all the works of charity he had created.

His having to take leave of his mother was both moving and full of sorrow. His mother, in saying goodbye to her son exclaimed: "I prefer to die without him than to see him in Rome unfaithful to his beliefs." From that day onward she was afflicted with a debilitating weakness, her movements became slower... She breathed and moved, but in her heart she was already dead. There is no doubt that she knew she would not see her son again except in heaven.

Meanwhile the coach drew further away, escorted by soldiers, taking Gaspar and his heroic companions to the calvary of exile and imprisonment, wherein the Lord would forge, out of his suffering, the future apostle of the Divine Blood.

PRISONER OF CHRIST

This exile and the inhuman imprisonment lasted from July 1810 to February 1814. Here are the stages of this journey: the cities of Piacenza, Bologna, Imola and Lugo. But before proceeding to the narration of some of the more memorable events, we must add as a preamble that, although Gaspar was the youngest in the group, it was he who encouraged the others and exhorted them to accept for love of the Church of Christ whatever suffering the hand of Providence offered them. The priests were treated very severely, completely isolated, forbidden to read or write and, hardest for them to bear, they were not allowed to celebrate Mass or receive Communion. Napoleon was playing for keeps!

When they reached Piacenza a number of them were put into the prison. Gaspar and Albertini were dropped off in a little square, where there was a dilapidated and filthy structure which passed for an inn. At their own expense they obtained a room which didn't even have a candle in it. However, they were fortunate enough to spend that first night in exile together, lying on two straw mattresses spread out on the floor. Gaspar couldn't get to sleep. Memories began to flood his mind and...his mother, his dear mother... Surely, she too, that night found it impossible to sleep.

All at once he began to hear strange guttural noises from Canon Albertini who was thrashing in his sleep next to him. "Don Francesco, don't you feel well? What is it? Why don't you say something?" In the total darkness he became very upset and yelled out for help. "I'm coming! I'm coming!" an old waiter answered, but he kept delaying. What had happened was that something slimy had caught in Albertini's throat as he slept with his mouth open and he was unable to either swallow it or spit it out. He was on the verge of suffocating. Finally he managed to cough up a huge mouse which spattered hard against the wall. When the old waiter finally arrived, he became quite angry: "For such a little thing you yell out for help?" Gaspar was so disgusted by the incident that for the rest of his life he had an inordinate fear of mice.

From the inn they went to the parish residence of St. Matthew where they paid for their lodgings. Gaspar was afflicted by an illness which became increasingly more serious and was accompanied by migraines, vomiting and fever. He was on the verge of expiring and the last rites were administered. Albertini decided it was time to reveal the secret to him. "You are not going to die, Don Gaspar. A nun..." He then proceeded to recount the prophesy and the great good he was destined to do for humanity. Gaspar was perplexed. He had complete faith in his confessor and spiritual director, but he found it hard to believe that the Lord would choose so insignificant a creature as himself to accomplish such great deeds. "You have accepted death in your heart and are resigned to the will of God. But his plans are not what you think and therefore you are not going to die." Albertini's words were followed by all the signs of a rapid recovery. The fever subsided, his stomach began to accept food and his strength and his cheeks became rosy once more.

His mother was not aware of her son's serious illness, nor did Gaspar know that his mother was slowly dying. But their hearts beat in unison and they knew...

THE LONG ORDEAL

Suddenly an order came down from above. Two hundred priests interned at Piacenza were to be transferred, some to Corsica and the others, many too old or in poor health, to Bologna.

The healthier air of this illustrious city and the comparative freedom of the first days spent there, where Gaspar was the guest of the Filippini Fathers (the room he slept in has been preserved intact) gave him the opportunity of writing to Rome. His first thoughts were for his family and the works he had left behind in the Capital. After spending several months with the Filippini Fathers, Gaspar went to stay with Albertini who was a guest of the noble family of the Bentivoglio. Here, on his insistence, he was housed in the attic in order to "have more freedom and peace to dedicate himself to prayer and the study of theology."

But Gaspar was a man of action and, having regained some measure of freedom, he now felt the fire that had burned in Rome begin to rekindle within him. He started preaching spiritual exercises, giving lectures to the young and imparting lessons on theology. He contacted the eminent teachers and the students of the renowned University. He distributed pamphlets among the students which refuted those materialistic doctrines that had led them away from the faith. The young Del Bufalo had found his paradise once more. But how could it last? Suddenly Don Francesco Gambini, one of his companions in exile, died; Gaspar managed to be at his side to hear his final gasp. The news spread all over the city and Gaspar, true to form, organized a solemn funeral. A confessor of the faith had died! The clergy of Bologna, two hundred exiled priests and an enormous crowd followed the coffin. The Chief of Police trembled, but Gaspar saw to it that there were no incidents.

HIS MOTHER DIES

We come now to the saddest and most painful part of the long period of detention. Gaspar heard the cruel news of his dear mother's death while he was in prison. Through those mysterious paths which those who love each other are able to find, Annunziata had learned about her son's serious illness, and Gaspar had heard of the precarious state of his mother's health. Annunzianta, on her death bed, almost smiling, murmured: "God's will be done! I shall see my Gaspar again in heaven." And with his name on her lips she went to meet her Maker on October 20, 1811. It was Albertini himself, before he left for Corsica, who undertook the painful task of breaking the news to him. He struggled to keep back the tears, but the law of the heart prevailed and he wept bitterly. He wrote the following to Sister Tamini: "To the other tribulations which the Lord has been pleased to visit upon me, has been added the loss of my saintly and incomparable mother. Although I accept the will of God, my human nature cannot help but feel the enormous weight caused by her absence...the wound is too fresh! I am stunned! The sorrow of my mother's death is inexpressible!" He ends on a note of heroic resignation: "Long live the Cross!"

The authorities were so irritated by the celebration of the funeral for Gambini, that the Chief of Police sent many of the two hundred priests to Corsica, among them Albertini, and locked the rest up in the Prison of St. Giovanni in Monte at Bologna. Gaspar was placed in solitary confinement. The authorities held the vain conviction that, by dividing them, it would be easier to weaken their influence.

The prison of St. Giovanni in Monte, where frequent revolts, accompanied by death and injury, had been the rule among the common criminals, now became a model prison thanks to the presence of Gaspar. The authorities were baffled! The good citizens of Bologna vied with each other in donating food and clean linen; Gaspar gave everything to the most hardened criminals, so he could talk to them about the love of Christ.

In the evening, from behind those walls a solemn chorus of voices could be heard singing praises to the Lord; indeed the prisoners, being somewhat superstitious and believing that they were chanting their own last rites in advance, put themselves into the singing, heart and soul. How can the song of those who are suffering be silenced by force when they praise the Lord who gives them the dignity to suffer for Him? Gaspar was perceived to represent a danger there and along with his companions he was transferred to the stricter prison facilities at Imola. The people there, having heard in advance of their arrival, went to meet them. Even though it was well known that the prisoners were forbidden to write and to celebrate mass, in some mysterious way the people were able to get the Eucharist in to them. The feats of St. Tarcisius were happening all over again! Every so often Mons. Ginasi would climb up to the Rock to celebrate the Holy Sacrifice and to distribute the Bread of the Angels to them. Later, when the restrictions were relaxed a little, they were all allowed to celebrate Mass. The harsh fortress of Imola was resplendent in the light that shone in the hearts of the people: those prisoners raised up for themselves and for the populace the consecrated Host and chalice.

After three months, having again refused to swear the oath of allegiance, the prisoners were transferred to the severe fortress of Lugo where a terrible prison guard named Lupo, in a gross abuse of his authority, put five people into each cell, deprived them of the most harmless objects, cut in half their already meagre and disgusting rations, stole personal family keepsakes from them and kept them from celebrating Mass or receiving Holy Communion.

Meanwhile matters were going badly for Napoleon.

At the beginning of December 1813 the political Administrator had left Lugo in a hurry. An order had been issued to have all the imprisoned priests transferred to Corsica. Gaspar, passing through Bologna where he had stayed on to take leave of his friends, decided to head for Florence and await events there. There he heard the happy news that Napoleon's star had set and that those who had been deported were free to return home.

Gaspar stayed on for a while and dedicated himself to preaching devotion to the Most Precious Blood. True, he was also anxious to return to Rome, but why hurry? His dear mother was no longer at home waiting for him!

He left in February 1814. When he caught sight of the Seven

Hills of Rome from his coach, amongst which Michelangelo's Cupola stood out, his heart burst with emotion and a torrent of tears came gushing from his eyes.

"Such a long journey in so short a time along the sublime path of the cross!" De Libero was to comment.

O. Scarpelli

HIS CHARISMA

Gaspar, apostle of the Most Precious Blood, in ecstasy before the Crucifix.

God, in His infinite mercy, had led him back home, imbued with the radiance of martyrdom. Were there triumphal celebrations, honours heaped upon him? Plum posts as a reward? Not at all. In Gaspar there burned only one desire: that of becoming an Apostle of Christ. He was certain that his suffering had not come to an end, that it was just beginning and destined to be ever harsher until the end of his life. He was about to embark on a new life: that of a Missionary and Apostle of the Most Precious Blood of Jesus.

Before seeing him in action, it might be better to present a brief description of Gaspar the man, both his physical characteristics and the interior life which spurred him on to accomplish such feats as were to transform the society of his time.

THE MAN

We do not have an actual portrait of the saint painted while he was alive. The closest thing we have is the one which is reproduced on the cover of this book. It is said that the painter of it got his description from an old woman who was devoted to the Saint and who made him do the picture over and over again until it reflected his soul. At last she exclaimed: "That is the Venerable Don Gaspar!" All later artists who have drawn his likeness have taken their inspiration from this one source. "Wide mouth, slightly turgid lips, somewhat wide–eyed with opal, perfectly round eyes – they always seemed to be enrapt at the sight of some lofty or abstruse thing. His face was full and rosy, always set in a serious and kind demeanour. He had a broad forehead and a sharp chin marred by the effects of smallpox. He had a fragile constitution. To look at him he seemed healthy enough, but he was always to suffer from the frailty which he had exhibited as a baby. To this were added the effects of the suffering he underwent during his exile, along with the penance he inflicted on himself and the hardships his apostolate imposed on him. All this contributed to his frequent bouts of nervousness, reddening in the face and bleeding gums." He was of average height, his bearing straightforward and modest, accompanied by a certain innate majesty. Thus, as already mentioned, he was often referred to as a born gentleman. His look was modest and his actions reserved and proper; his gentleness won over even the most unruly of souls. He was very conscientious, docile and at the same time energetic, tireless and open–minded. His "way of doing things was very serious, but kind and affable, as is is befitting a Minister of God." (Merlini)

Though he was by nature "impetuous, fiery, fervid, bilious, excitable, tending towards the irascible, restless, hot–tempered", he was successful, through continuous union with God, in mastering himself completely and gaining such control that he became the most peaceful and gentlest of men. "He suffered with indifference and worked with joy." "We must become aware of difficulties," he would say, "and not to be afraid of or give in to them." He was endowed with a keen intelligence which he put to use but never vaunted. He suffered constantly from stomach trouble but he neither complained, nor allowed anyone to prepare anything special for him to eat. He kept his suffering to himself with surprising alacrity. He was poor in the extreme, yet always neat: his clothes might be mended but never dirty. Whoever went into his room was struck by the extreme cleanliness, neatness and simplicity. When he could, he did his own cleaning and tidying up.

He was the sworn enemy of idleness. He would not indulge in visits or conversations unless they were necessary and useful.

To those who advised him to take some rest he answered: "I will rest in heaven."

His spirit was capable of remaining unperturbed despite the criticism, the censure, the contradictions, the scathing slander and the struggles he had to face daily in order to defend the glory of God and his own Institution. He was truly a man of strength who did not give in when confronted by difficulties, no matter how insurmountable they seemed. He forgave his enemies and prayed for them. Even during his period of imprisonment, he was never heard to utter one single word of resentment or condemnation aimed at Napoleon or his jailers.

Another of Gaspar's characteristics was his spiritual sensitivity which revealed the gentleness of his soul. He would say: "I love everyone in God and through God, without distinction." He adapted to all kinds of people even if, clearly, he preferred to spend his time with the poor and those who had sinned. "His physical make–up seems to have been created for the very purpose of feeling to the core the moral, spiritual and physical miseries of his fellow man," Cardinal Giusmini used to say. He was very kind with those who had sinned and even when he had to correct or discipline his missionaries he did everything with such gentleness and fatherly solicitude that the guilty were easily and readily won over. Sinners felt overwhelmed and, after having experienced his goodness, they arose from his feet weeping with joy. Even priests would flock in large numbers to listen to him going through the Spiritual Exercises and he not only spoke with them, preached and heard confessions, but he would also perform the most menial tasks for them.

Even after he had been in prison he observed this way of life which Albertini had taught him. He would rise very early, recite his morning prayers, scrupulously prepare himself to celebrate Mass and to give thanks. Witnesses commonly reported that when he celebrated mass he did it with such concentration and miraculous devotion that he looked like an angel. The crowds always flocked in great numbers "to hear the mass of an angel." He was a strict observer of the Rule which he himself had given his Missionaries. He was devoted to Meditation which he engaged in constantly and he would stand before the Crucifix for hours on end meditating on the Passion of Christ. During the day he would often recite short prayers. He never missed reciting the Breviary, even when he could have received dispensation from doing so.

He would attend to his duties with admirable order and

O. Scarpelli

precision and repeated often the words of the Apostle: "Let everything be done in an orderly and honest manner."

He ate simple food and drank little wine. In fact he drank wine with water in it. Before and after his long sermons, he would drink hot orgeat (a drink made from barley). He would usually mete out the portions at meals and he always served himself last and sparingly. He disapproved of excess and forbade rare or costly delicacies, but he would reprimand those responsible if the table was not supplied with wholesome and sufficient food. During special days he would always see to it that there was something extra special to eat. Even when ill, he respected the fasts required by the Church and added others of his own free will. At the Mission he was strict in not allowing choice foods, sweets or liqueurs and if any of these were received as a gift he would have them immediately distributed among the poor. Once during a Mission his lay brother had received a nice cake as a gift and kept it hidden because he knew he could not accept it. He showed it only when they were back at the Mission House but Gaspar ordered him to take it to the hospital immediately. To those Missionaries who were unable to observe these rules because of ill–health he would say: "Stay home until you are well." He never accepted invitations from prelates or nobles. He would rarely go out for walks, preferring to visit a church or a hospital.

He didn't sleep more than five hours; and it was not unusual for him to spend the night answering the enormous amount of correspondence or praying. Sometimes he didn't even get into bed, but he would unmake it so that the others would not know he had not slept. His companions put pins in his sheets to see whether he had gone to bed or not, in the morning they would find them exactly where they had put them.

"To speak little, to speak well and to speak when appropriate" was the maxim he lived by. When he walked with his companions or during recreation, he would begin talking about God and never stop. He was very reserved in his behaviour and modest

Pius VII authorizes Gaspar to found the new Congregation dedicated to the Most Precious Blood of Jesus.

in his glance. He encouraged his friends to behave likewise and to those who complained that this kind of life was rather hard he would say: "God will give us the strength and grant us the grace."

His steadfastness was most noticeable in adversity. We will refer later on to the many hardships he encountered in founding his Congregation, in reforming the Church, in converting the brigands and in spreading the cult of devotion to the Most Precious Blood. Seeing his companions discouraged and disheartened, he would urge them on by saying: "Don't lose heart! It is the Work of God, God will help us." "Patience is the sign of the apostle. We must make sacrifices for the glory of God."

It is clear, even from the little we have said, that Gaspar structured his entire life around humility and the suffering of the Cross. He knew that human glory and the search for satisfaction in recognition from other human beings is an impediment to the soul's sublime flight towards the high summits of sanctity. He thought of himself as a sinner and as useless, a mere instrument, the "tool" in the hands of the Lord to be used to accomplish whatever He wanted of him. "To God the Glory, to me the contempt!" For this reason he preferred humble places, because it is there that the humble are to be found, the souls which are most dear to God. Convinced that with humility one could be victorious over the pride of one's ego, he never let an occasion slip by without practising it. If he was praised, he left, if he was reprimanded he bowed his head, if his saintliness was extolled he proclaimed himself to be the most abject of sinners. "If others had received the gifts given to me by God, they would be great saints. I wonder if I'll even be saved!" He did not like high office and honours and declined to become a Bishop, a Papal Nuncio or a Cardinal.

From these few notes, it appears that Gaspar was complete as a man, both physically and spiritually. Or, as he has been defined, the man and the saint of equilibrium, mature enough to accomplish things that are out of the ordinary. During his youth, while in prison, and in his future actions, he was to show himself to be a great organizer. His eloquence made him stand out but he used it only to preach of the Crucified Christ, never out of vanity. He was introverted by nature, he loved retreats, prayer, and the solitude of his Houses. But his life, to the day of his death, was to be one continuous act of charity. The times, the priesthood, the responsibilities he shouldered, all of these imposed on him many tasks that were unpleasant. But he loved and forgave a great deal and through this gift of forgiveness he was blessed with the joy of the saints. In a century filled with hatred, with struggles, with social climbing at any cost, Gaspar went out from the narrow doors of the churches, descended onto the squares and like a tribune of God he addressed the crowds, lashed out at vice, redeemed souls for God, brought peace to the people and re–established the balance which vice and hatred had destroyed. "To make of him a saint," a biographer has said, "the goodness of this man of God would suffice, a goodness which is both on the inside and the outside, always silently operating towards his friends and those who did him harm, a human and religious goodness. A goodness which is a sign of having attained the greatest wisdom and equilibrium. In the Gospel such men are called: Just." (L. Santandrea)

HIS SPIRITUAL LIFE

Before examining further Gaspar's long and marvellous journey as an apostle, we must look at his inner nature because no one can bring to fruition such saintly, exalted and prodigious feats unless he is endowed with a flame, a special charisma, an ideal which burns bright in his soul.

There is something extraordinary about us Christians which is particularly evident in the lives of the saints, and that is that even though we have the same faith, even though we love the same Christ, the driving force of life in each of us can have an energy all its own. The Saints differ from each other in the extraordinary richness and variety of their works, yet they live in the same Lord Christ.

St. Gaspar has been compared to John the Evangelist for his ever present purity, for the heights reached by his eloquence, for his trusting devotion at the foot of the Cross. Here, like John, he will be captivated, enthralled by the Crucifix and enamoured of the Blood which runs in streams from the wounds and the side of Jesus. His saintly mother had set him on the path towards this

O. Scarpelli

Precious Blood, and he had savoured it for the first time at his First Communion. He saw it gushing forth after the words of the Consecration every morning from the chalice of his Mass. In the horror of prison the transports of love for that Most Precious Blood confirmed him in his readiness to give his own blood for Christ who had shed it for all of us; there he was to learn that he would be the founder of a Congregation which would bear that most holy name and that he, for the rest of his life, would raise that scarlet banner before the peoples and the nations. He, like John before the cross, would be accompanied by the holiness and the sublime purity of Mary and the tears of contrition of thousands of sinners like Magdalen.

Having set out on the scarlet path of that Blood and sustained by the concept of universal Redemption which It expresses and puts into action, he drew the inspiration for his life from It, because the meditation on the martyrdom of Christ carried him beyond the usual and common duties of a priest. From this meditation arose the desire to bring that Blood of Redemption to all souls and he became its greatest apostle.

He who was so detached from the world, in order that even the things which were most dear to him might not restrict any part of his devotion for Christ to whom he had already given himself completely, received from that Blood the drive to go forth and embrace his fellow men and bring to them the love of Christ. He was conscious of the fact that an apostle of that Blood is not allowed to live in lofty solitude; he must, as the Master did, remain among the people who thirst after redemption and forgiveness. Gaspar, like John, would make use of that Heart from which the Blood of Redemption overflows in scarlet waves: the Heart is the well–spring of that Blood.

Gaspar's soul, filled to the brim with so much wealth, which constitutes the greatest among the themes of spirituality, trembled with the desire to rush wherever there was a need for total self–sacrifice; he could not keep the propulsive force of his charity in check. The Blood is not a treasure to keep locked up

On August 15, 1815 Gaspar with his first companions opens the first House of the new Institute at St.Felice di Giano in Umbria.

in the secret cavities of one's soul; the Blood is oblivious to obstacles, it breaks through, overflows and envelops those who receive it until they become sated and transmit it to others in their turn. This is why the desire to act was so strong in Gaspar that it led him to give all of himself and even beyond himself in a manner which is scarcely believable, as we shall see.

His were times in which Europe was shaken and dyed red with the blood which Napoleon shed with his wars, times in which a war "was waged not against this dogma or that one, but against religion in its totality and against the Crucified Christ. It is necessary, then, to reproduce the glories of the Cross and of the Crucifix...it is necessary to tell the people once again at what price souls are redeemed... it is necessary remind people that this Blood is offered every morning on the altar."

"This Blood is administered during the sacraments...it is the price of salvation...the token of Divine Love." "We ecclesiastics have received the sacrament of priesthood in order that we may administer the Divine Blood to souls." "This is a devotion which derives from what we have in Holy Scripture." "You have redeemed us, Lord, with your Blood!... This is a fundamental devotion which embraces all others; it is the basis, the supporting structure, the essence of Catholic piety... Devotion to the Most Precious Blood: this is the weapon for the times."

Gaspar made a vow to become its propagator. He never preached a sermon in which he did not mention the love with which Christ had shed His Blood for all our souls. The principal goal of the Congregation bearing the name of the Most Precious Blood, he wrote in the Rule, was to be the cult and the propagation of devotion to the Blood of Christ. He dedicated a great deal of time meditating on this Mystery and to prayer. Before the Crucifix, "he would become all inflamed and often he was transfixed in ecstasy." In the Blood of Jesus were all his comfort and hope. "The devil would devour me if it weren't for a wreath of chalices which I seem to see encircling my spirit." One day while preaching on the Most Precious Blood in the open, he didn't stop even though he was drenched to the bone. In all the priests, even in those who were going on Missions abroad, he instilled this devotion and gave them the tools through which they might propagate it. On the doors of houses and of rooms he would have people write the following: MAY THE DIVINE BLOOD LIVE ON! In the Missions he instituted the Confraternity of the Most Precious Blood and the Hour of Perpetual Adoration of the Blood of Christ. The more moving rituals were those of the Stations of the Cross, of the Procession of the Dead Christ, of the Little Crown of the Most Precious Blood, of the Seven Offerings and the observance of the Month in Honour of the Most Precious Blood. Twelve churches in Rome took turns and devoted one month each in making this last observence, thus ensuring that it occurred all year round without interruption.

He would exhort his missionaries in the following manner: "Go forth and take the Blood of Christ to the whole world."

QUEEN OF THE MOST PRECIOUS BLOOD

"In his heart and in his apostolic Mission, his devotion to the Blood of Jesus was one with his devotion to Mary." Is not the Blood of Jesus, Mary's Blood also? Had he not seen in Roman icons, as a boy, the eyes moving "in which all of heaven is contained"? As a youth he would drag his friends to visit the numerous churches dedicated to the Virgin; as a Missionary he never neglected to visit the main sanctuaries. In the Marche he visited the Holy House of Loreto several times and there he saw visions, received prophetic messsages and comfort. He was among the proudest and most enthusiastic supporters of the Mystery of the Immaculate Conception of Mary and, as we shall see, he insisted on inaugurating his Congregation on August 15, a day sacred to the Assumption of Maria Mary in Heaven He wrote: "She will protect it from heaven and bless it with her love."

To show that Mary was indissolubly linked as Co–redemptress to the Mystery of the Divine Blood, he commissioned a painting in which we see the Virgin holding the Child Jesus who is holding a Chalice of His Blood while she, with an open hand, invites the devout to meditate upon that Blood and pray for strength. He would exhibit that painting to be venerated during the Missions and he maintained that the Mission began from that very moment because "it was Our Lady who gave meaning to the Mission."

The sermon on "our Divine Mother" moved everyone to tears and it was impossible to keep count of all the conversions. The individual gifts of grace received and the miracles performed through the intercession of the Virgin of the Most Precious Blood were many, as we discover. It was not unusual to see rays of light emanating from the painting and enveloping the saint. Mary was the "conqueror of the heart". It is reported that the Virgin said to a pious soul, perhaps Merlini, that Gaspar was the apple of her eye.

ST. FRANCIS XAVIER

At the beginning of this book we mentioned the special grace received with regard to young Gaspar's sight through the intercession of St. Francis Xavier. From that moment on there burned in him the flame of grateful love and devotion which he nurtured all his life. Gaspar took St. Francis as a model for his life as a Missionary, emulating his great zeal. He propagated devotion to him, distributing images and commissioning paintings of him. In the churches of the Congregation there was always either an altar or the simulacrum of the Crucifix, Our Lady of the Most Precious Blood and that of St. Francis Xavier. He chose him as patron of the Institute. He solemnly celebrated his Feast day on December 3 and the week before the Feast he would invite the Missionaries to gather in spiritual exercises. He always instilled in his followers and in the people a strong devotion toward the Apostle of the Indies. He also instituted a male confraternity called the "Big Brothers of St. Francis Xavier".

He tried to send at least one Missionary to continue the apostolate of the Saint in Goa because he didn't want his missionaries not to be present where so great an apostle had been. But he was unable to fulfill this desire. That dream is becoming a reality today. In fact, the first House of the

Gaspar improvises as a bricklayer and carpenter in the restoration of the old convent of St. Felix.

Missionaries of the Most Precious Blood in India has been opened where local nuns of the order of the Adorers of the Blood of Christ have been working for some time.

FOUNDER

Having returned to Rome from prison, Gaspar took up where he had left off with his religious and charitable work and, alongside Albertini, gave himself entirely to the Archconfraternity of the Most Precious Blood in St. Nicola in Carcere. Sincerely convinced in his humility that he was not capable of fulfilling Sister Agnese's prophesy, when he learned that the Company of Jesus had been reconstituted he asked, along with his friend, Carlo Odescalchi, to be admitted to it. As can be imagined, he was received with open arms. But God had other plans; not even a day passed when they both received an invitation to appear before the Pope who, without mincing words, ordered Gaspar to dedicate himself totally to the Work of the Missions, going even so far as to exonerate him of his duties as a Canon. He ordered Odescalchi, instead, to prepare himself for a diplomatic career. In fact he was later to become a Cardinal and remained a friend of the Saint. Still not convinced that he was the one pre–ordained to be the founder of the Congregation, Gaspar joined a group of missionary priests directed by Don Gaetano Bonanni, giving Don Gaetano credit for everything accomplished: for himself, he was satisfied with spreading devotion to the Most Precious Blood and dedicating himself passionately to the task of preaching. It was not long however, before God's will began to be realized.

Bonanni had gathered about him a number of priests who, after preaching, would go back to their own homes. Gaspar, however, dreamt of a new Institute, an undertaking which would survive him over time. Soon an opportunity arose of opening the first House at Toscanella, in Lazio, but everything fell through because of the indecision of Bonanni. From the very beginning of Gaspar's apostolate, the Lord had given him a marvellous gift: the friendship of Mons. Bellisario Cristaldi, who was to become his guardian angel, his protector and his benefactor throughout his life. It was he who helped him to open the first

House of the new Institute.

In fact, he invited Gaspar to accompany him to Giano in Umbria in the diocese of Spoleto to preach a triduum for the Feast of All Saints and All Souls. Many spiritual benefits arose following the sermons. Such peace, thought Gaspar, such sanctity emanating from the sweet land of Umbria. In a hurried tour of those beguiling hills, he happened upon an ancient and imposing monastery: St. Felix! It's true that it was almost in ruins and would need vast renovations since it had been long abandoned by the Passionists; but his heart beat as though he had discovered a regal palace and he dreamt of opening there the first House of the new Institute.

November 30, 1814 became an unforgettable date for Gaspar and his future brothers: Pius VII granted Gaspar the church, the convent and the attached structures of St. Felix as well as an annual pension and permission to open the first House of the new Congregation to bear the name of the Most Precious Blood of Christ.

With exquisite sensitivity and much humility Gaspar had the grant awarded to Bonanni. On the heels of such joy followed a painful setback. Bonanni, informed of the location and the dilapidated condition of the buildings, firmly refused to go. And, for one reason or another, so did all his other companions, even though they had initially spoken warmly of Gaspar's idea. It was one thing to be away from Rome for a few days to preach and then to return to the comfort of one's own home; it was quite another to abandon everything, to leave Rome for a life full of hardship in a monastery at St. Felix far from home. Gaspar, obstinate in letting others have the limelight, entreated Tonnelli to go there in place of Bonanni. But he, too, overwhelmed by the difficulties that would be encountered, refused to go. As always happens in the works of God, alongside those who refused there were those who began speaking ill, accusing Gaspar of being proud and inept. Here began the martyrdom which was to accompany the Saint to his death bed. But it was also here that his rallying cry took form: "It is the work of God. He will look after it!" Only one man remained steadfastly at his side: Cristaldi! And Gaspar admitted to him: "Excellency, everyone has pulled out! I will be a Missionary on my own!"

The first results of such courage were not long in coming. Gaspar, with his patience and his tenacity succeeded in convincing Bonanni to at least go with him to take possession of the convent. Pius VII received them, blessed them and encouraged them; then Gaspar set off alone, followed by Bonanni. It is said that the latter, upon seeing the state of St. Felix, finally understood Gaspar's heroism, threw himself at his feet and wept. Shortly afterwards, they were joined by the others.On August 15, 1815, the first House of the new Congregation was finally and officially opened with great solemnity. Everyone recognized Gaspar as being its sole and indisputable Founder.

The event attracted the good people of Umbria from the surrounding valleys, from the villages and from the towns. Great was their joy as they gathered with faith and enthusiasm to hear the Missionaries sing the "Te Deum". Gaspar informed Cristaldi of it immediately relating even the minutest details, beginning his letter as follows: "It would be more appropriate to write this with tears of tenderness than with ink."

THE CONGREGATION
OF THE MOST PRECIOUS BLOOD

Such joy was quickly followed by many thorns. His enemies immediately began their perverse whisper campaigns in order to stifle the Institute just as it was being born; so vehement were these attacks that Gaspar, whether out of humility or in order to save it, let it be known that the founder was Pius VII. To avoid dangerous confusion, the Missionaries, first among them being Don Giovanni Merlini, urged Gaspar to allow the truth to be known. Gaspar finally consented.

In the records of the Trial for the beatification and canonization of St. Gaspar, kept in the Holy Congregation of the Rites,

Don Valenti, unable to meet the payments to his creditors, is exhorted by Gaspar to count once more the coins in the bowl and watches as the money multiplies miraculously in his hands.

Merlini's arguments showed beyond a doubt that Gaspar was the true and only founder of the Congregation of the Missionaries of the Most Precious Blood, with the permission, obviously, of Pius VII. Albertini was the founder of the Archconfraternity of the Most Precious Blood at St. Nicola in Carcere in Rome and Bonanni was the Director of a group of priests who, while remaining with their own families, dedicated themselves to the Missions to the people. The founder of the Congregation, then, was none other than St. Gaspar! Conclusive evidence of this lies in the fact that it was he who first gave it its name and then staunchly defended it; it was he who opened and closed the various Houses as the need dictated; it was he who chose, admitted or expelled its members and decided where they would live and what their duties would be. It was he, in fact, who dealt with the Ecclesiastical Departments and the Bishops; he who determined the Ministries and founded the Colleges. And, finally, with the help of Merlini, it was he who wrote the Rule of the Congregation.

Now that this important fact about the life of the Saint has been established, let us look briefly at the nature of his Congregation.

From the very beginning it was his intention to create an Institute of Lay Priests who, although they took no vows, were united by the common bond of charity, defined by St. Paul as the "bond of perfection". These priests were to dedicate themselves to the preaching of the Missions to the people and spread the worship of and devotion to the Most Precious Blood; thus the Institute was to be called "Congregation of the Missionaries of the Most Precious Blood of Our Lord Jesus Christ". We emphasize here the thought of the Saint which we alluded to in the chapter on the devotion to the Most Precious Blood.

"If other Institutes take it upon themselves to disseminate this or that devotion, ours must undertake to spread the one devotion which contains within it all of the others, that is: the price of our Redemption."

"This name derives from what we find in Holy Scripture: 'You have redeemed us, O Lord, with Your Blood and You have made of us a Kingdom for our God and our priests.' We ecclesiastics, then, receive the sacrament of holy orders so that we may administer the Divine Blood to all souls. This Blood is offered through the Divine Sacrifice, and is administered through the sacraments; it is the Price of Redemption and what we can offer to our Heavenly Father as redemption for sinners. In this devotion we have the treasures of Wisdom and of Holiness; in it are our comfort, our peace and our salvation."

This is also the thought of Mons. Cristaldi which Gaspar repeats in a "Post Scriptum" to a letter to Don Gaetano Bonanni dated March 1, 1815:

"Mons. Cristaldi urges me do our work in the name of the Most Precious Blood of Jesus. He makes the following observation. Those who do Evangelical work, do so by ensuring that the Blood of Jesus is used to save Souls, and they must do this continuously, asking that sinners be forgiven; thus, if other Institutes devote themselves to propagating this or that particular devotion, this Institute of the Missions must undertake to spread that one devotion which includes within it all the others, that is: the Price of our Redemption."

Gaspar, then, had no intention at all of founding a religious order. Instead, he wanted only to gather, under the banner of the Blood of Christ, a community of priests ready to go wherever they were needed to preach the Holy Missions to the people and thereby to dedicate themselves to the conversion of souls to God. Being a part of the Institute was, therefore, voluntary and whoever might have had second thoughts could choose to leave of his own free will. The members, having to devote themselves exclusively to the preaching of the Missions and to running the Churches of the Institute, were obliged to live where they were posted. Gaspar insisted that harmony should prevail amongst the individual members and between superiors and subordinates, in order that peace, serenity, respect, tolerance and happiness might flourish amongst them. He urged everyone to help each other and not to transfer from house to house that which was displeasing. "Let each one of us live like an angel incarnate and be an example of goodness to others; let us be joyful, sociable and courteous, because courtesy is a virtue, and let us all dress and speak with decorum."

Gaspar went so far as to take charge of the minutest details regarding the quality and quantity of the food consumed and,

like an affectionate father toward his children, he worried about their health, their comfort, their sleep...Of course his Rule was primarily concerned with the spiritual life of the Missionary, beginning with the way he celebrated mass, the practice of piety, retreats and spiritual Exercises, the reciting of the Breviary and the daily examination of one's conscience.

Then there were detailed instructions on the life lived in common and for the Holy Mysteries. The Missionary, not having taken vows of poverty, was allowed to own private assets and dispose of them as he wished. Gaspar counselled those who had assets to donate them to the poor and also to assist the Congregation since it, too, was poor. He regulated with extreme precision and rigour the division of that which was earned by the Ministries or that which was received in performing one's duty as a Missionary, from that which was derived from the personal property of individual members.

The complex regulations of his Rule reveal the keenness of his insight. It seems that nothing eluded him insofar as the vocation and fidelity to the divine calling were concerned and this is reflected in the prudent nature of the provisions which did so much to safeguard and strengthen that calling. He was not being pedantic, merely prudent and balanced. He also included detailed instructions on the Sacrament of Confession. We will speak later on of the Method of the Holy Missions. Here we will limit ourselves to adding that he wanted the greatest decorum to prevail in the Churches of the Institute and he stipulated there was to be a raised platform rather than a pulpit so that the preacher would have greater contact with his audience, who, he urged, should be addressed with simple persuasiveness and spoken to of the Crucified Christ.

He was very concerned that the Houses be provided with all that was necessary, that the greatest order and cleanliness should prevail and that all luxuries and useless appurtenances should be forbidden. He dictated how one should behave in case of

Such was the poverty of the Institute, that when it rained, they had to share an umbrella among three people.

sickness or death. He insisted that each House contain archives in which documents, records, chronicles and all important acts concerning the Congregation and individual House Chapters were to be scrupulously kept. The Rule set down the dress code of the fathers, the lay brothers and the aspiring priests. The fathers were always to wear a cassock with a sash, even at home, and a reasonably large crucifix on their chests hanging from a gold–plated chain. They were to wear a skull cap and a hat away from home as Roman custom dictated.

The members of the Institute were not weighed down with penances, fasts, or rituals of piety performed in common. Those prescribed by the Church were sufficient for all. A few prayers in common and meditation were required, along with a brief examination of conscience twice a day. The women were to be strictly cloistered.

In the whole of St. Gaspar's Rule great care was taken to avoid oppression, to simplify and alleviate, leaving each member the greatest possible freedom is compatible with a life in common. The House was to be like a nest to which the Missionary yearned to return between his forays into the world, a place where he could find brotherhood and be restored in order to meet the challenges of a new apostolic undertaking.

He wanted his Missionaries to be pious, but also learned and he insisted that their education be serious and up–to–date. He ensured that there would be daily study groups in all the Houses on the various ecclesiastical disciplines and made readings at meals mandatory. Each house was to have a well–stocked, modern library.

We have looked briefly at the Rule and examined the structure of the new Congregation. But we know from Merlini that the Rule was not the product of a few days' work. It was the fruit of years of study, first–hand experience and prayer. The Saint would dictate the rules as the necessity arose and he would constantly revise and improve on them in the light of practice and continuous experimentation. In 1822 he gave Merlini and Don Biagio Valentini the task of drafting a compendium of the various regulations he had drawn up over the years, which he then revised and had published. On matters which needed immediate practical attention, he issued circulars which were to serve as guide lines for the Missionaries. To those who advised him to draw up a formal Rule, he would answer that he was in no hurry and would wait "until God sent it to him". And thus matters stood until 1835 when he dictated it to Merlini and had it written up "in proper Latin' by the missionary, Don Cristoforo Frioli.

The Rule is the quintessence of the evangelic spirit of the Saint, inspired primarily by charity. Of note is his concern not to impose duties of an absolute nature, but to respect the individual's freedom in fulfilling his obligations, as we have already mentioned. The Rule also gives us the measure of St. Gaspar's canonical knowledge which he used to formulate the fundamental structure of a Work which was to endure through the hardships and the blows of the times. He informs it with his balanced nature, his humility, his saintliness and his incomparable love of the Blood of Christ.

The Rule of the Congregation of the Missionaries of the Most Precious Blood is the testament of a great Saint.

Gaspar, writing to Cristaldo immediately following the opening of the First House at St. Felix of Giano, said: "The observance [of the Rule] was put immediately into effect." This statement makes it clear that Gaspar was a good manager because, after all the anxieties and difficulties involved in founding the Congregation, his first thought was to make it function as it should, for the good of the Church and the members themselves.

To what we have already mentioned, we must add the fact that he was so sure that the Congregation was the result of the will of God that he never faltered, even in the face of the greatest difficulties. He always encouraged his followers and defended it with all his might even when, on a practical level, everything and everyone seemed to be against him. He wanted the Congregation to live in poverty and whatever it might ask, it was to ask on behalf of the poor. "Should the day ever come when the Congregation no longer brings glory to God, on that day I shall no longer love it." "If the Congregation should ever become rich, I shall no longer recognize it as my own." This is why he refused generous offers and considerable legacies. With so many friends, with the enthusiasm of the public, with the

sympathy of the rich, he could easily have accumulated large sums; but he was born poor, he lived in poverty and he wanted to die poor. He wanted his Missionaries to be poor also. God rewarded him, as we shall see, by never allowing the bare necessities to be lacking. When people pointed out that the requests for Missions were many but the members of the Institute were few, he would answer: "The works of God never fail." And he would add: "God performs miracles for our Institute." To those who were recalcitrant and could not get used to the life of the Community and had entered it expecting to find ease and comfort there, he would repeat: "God does not have need of us. It is through grace that we are allowed to serve him in the Institute. If there is no obedience, there is no order. That is our way, and if there are those for whom it is not convenient, the door is always open." To some he said: "The devil will never stop harassing your vocation... you must trust in the Blood of Christ." "He was," Merlini relates, "very patient in instructing me in all matters relating to the Institute, even the most minute ones."

He was a very prudent administrator, never considering personal ambitions in the least. He refused all honours and appointments in order to dedicate himself exclusively to the Institute and to his apostolate. He never played favourites and in assigning duties and responsibilities he considered only what was good for and required by the Congregation and at the capabilities of the individual involved. He did everything in the light of God, "Who," he used to say, "will pass judgement on me." That is why he would make a decision only after lengthy prayer and after having celebrated Mass. Of the thousands of letters he wrote, the majority of them deal with the administration of the Institute and show how important to him were its development, the observance of the Rule, prudent administration and the spiritual and physical well–being of each member.

He so loved his Congregation that when he mentioned it he would doff his hat. Paraphrasing the Biblical exhortation, he

For several weeks the Community at St. Felix had been without wine. Gaspar blessed an empty barrel and excellent wine poured from it.

would often exclaim: "Let my right hand wither away, if I forget you, O Congregation of the Most Precious Blood."

HIS EARLIEST COMPANIONS

Gaspar Del Bufalo, Don Gaetano Bonanni, the marquis Don Vincenzo Tani, and Don Adriano Giampredi were the first four to be associated under the name of the Precious Blood of Jesus. Soon there would be others. According to Don Enrico Rizzoli, who has written brief biographies of these first companions of the Saint, they all possessed extraordinary virtue, so much so that each on his own was worthy of being venerated at the altar. To follow some one so persecuted as Gaspar was, living as they did a life so full of hardships, was truly an act of courage. But it was precisely this arduous existence, aside from the charisma of its Founder, which led these chosen few to make their choice. "Their story." Santandrea points out, "is worthy of being placed alongside that of the Little Flowers of St. Francis."

We will mention only a few here.

The marquis *Don Vincenzo Tani* was a straightforward man of simple habits and led a life of self–mortification and charity. After having met Gaspar, he renounced the comforts of the Palace to follow him. He was a strong promoter of devotion to Our Lady. He had the gift of reading into people's consciences and one day he went up to a young man and exhorted him to "cleanse" his conscience through confession. The fellow was so enraged that he gave him a sound beating!...Don Vincenzo, kneeling at his feet, merely kept saying over and over: "For pity's sake, save your soul!" Finally the young man knelt beside him and confessed. Tani was the first brother of the new Congregation to die. "A good sign," Gaspar said. "A saint has gone to meet God, the first to wear our uniform."

Don Gaetano Bonanni, whom we have already mentioned, after the controversy over St. Felix, realized that he had been wrong and remained there with such fervour that he came to refer to it as "paradise". He collaborated for a number of years with Gaspar until he was appointed Bishop of Nurcia. His office was merely a continuation of his missionary life. He was a very affable and simple man. He was conversant with neither money nor playing cards. Once, he went to visit the study area of the seminarians, who, rather than dedicating themselves to their studies were having a game of cards. Caught by surprise, they tried to hide the cards among the pages of their books. But they were not quick enough and left a nine [a figure mounted on a horse] on the table. The Bishop asked which saint the picture represented. "St. George!" came the ready reply. He turned and addressed all of them saying: "A great Saint indeed. Be firm in your devotion to him." And he kissed the image on the card. He gave all he had to the poor and when he died not even a shirt was found in his drawers. Everyone, even the enemies of the Church, called him the Holy Bishop.

Don Vincenzo Fontana. Gaspar used to say of him: "Although he is not a good preacher, he inspires others by the saintliness of his conduct." He was so eager to become part of the Congregation, ready even to be a servant, that Gaspar took him in, although because of his corpulence and his habits he was not cut out for the life of a missionary. His appetite was enormous, so much so that to satisfy it used to gather up all the old crusts of bread left over from the day before. He was extremely observant of the Rule and, what is truly remarkable, he, like all the others, climbed mountains and crossed rivers. He would go to the crossroads and exhort the people to go to listen to the sermons of the missionaries. He inspired so much confidence that he was much sought after as a confessor. He was very devoted to and a great apostle of the Most Precious Blood and of the Virgin. He died with a smile on his lips, looking upon the image of the Our Lady.

Don Biagio Valentini. We have already spoken of him and will have occasion to do so again. He was the first to succeed Gaspar in running the Congregation. His was a singular vocation and opposed at every turn by his relatives. He was invited by Gaspar to come to one of the Proselytizing Missions and once there, advised him to become a missionary. He was seriously ill with consumption and therefore, not suited to a life in a community filled with deprivations. Everyone advised him against it and surmised that either Gaspar was unaware of his state of health or that he had made a gross error in judgement. But Gaspar persevered, insisting that he would not suffer at all but

that, on the contrary, he would derive much joy from it. He asked him to come pray with him in the Holy House at Loreto and took him along on a Mission. Don Biagio could not believe what was happening to him, because he immediately felt at home and his health improved so much that he became enamoured of the life of the missionary. We shall recount later how his mother died. Eye witnesses have testified that he "resurrected" a child who was lifeless after falling into a well; he converted an obstinate non–believer just before the condemned man was to be executed; at Frosinone he brought a little girl back to life. As Gaspar had predicted to him, Don Biagio became his first successor and had the joy, not only of inaugurating the first Mission House in Rome, but also of seeing the Rule of the Institute approved by Gregory XVI on December 17, 1841.

Don Giovanni Merlini. We have already mentioned him and will speak of him again and of the part he played in the Institute. Without a doubt, he was the greatest emulator of Gaspar's holiness. It would be better to say that he was the shining and faithful mirror of his soul. He was even held to be more saintly than the Founder. He went from his native Spoleto to Giano to meet him and to join him in the holy Spiritual Exercises, without the least intention of becoming a missionary. He was overcome by Gaspar's spirituality and Gaspar in turn was captivated by the candour and the spiritual and intellectual gifts which Merlini possessed. It was the meeting of two great souls destined to journey together along the same path for the good of the Church. Merlini soon became Gaspar's secretary and confessor, his companion in the Missions, and his collaborator and most faithful follower in the work that was the Saint's calling. He put the Rule into practice and increased the Institute's numbers both in Italy and abroad. Pius IX regarded him highly, was extremely fond of him and chose him to be among his counsellors. The universal celebration of the Feast of the Most Precious Blood by the Church is due to him. When Pius IX was exiled to Gaeta following the insurrections of 1848, he predicted that if he

Gaspar in the den of the brigands among the mountains of southern Lazio.

extended the Feast of the Most Precious Blood to the Church at large, he would be able to return to Rome and indeed, this came to pass.

Don Giovanni was a particularly gifted shaper of souls. To him, as we shall mention later on, Gaspar entrusted the spiritual guidance of the young Maria De Mattias, who was to become the founder of the Institute of the Adorers of the Blood of Christ. She, in turn, faithfully followed the counsel and orders received. He made of her a chosen soul, endowed with such virtue that she reached the highest pinnacle of holiness.

His consummate skill as an orator won many souls to God. One of his Missions remained famous in Aquila. Among his many conquests was that of a brash young man who had gone astray. He had made fun of the Missionaries, but on the morning of their departure he ran after Don Giovanni and insisted that Giovanni hear his confession along the way. He ended up by becoming a member of the Institute that very day and remained in it all his life, leading an exemplary existence. Merlini was a little deaf but through the prayers of Gaspar he was able to hear very well during confession and spiritual conversations. He died at quite an advanced age through, an act of hatred against the faith in Rome, on January 12, 1873, when he was deliberately run over by a coachman who hated priests.

Pope Pius IX, when he heard of the news of his death, said in a public audience: "It is a great loss to the Church when the Lord calls to Himself souls such as those of Don Giovanni."

Although he was by temperament quite irascible, there was no one who was more meek and mild than he; he was fervent in his faith and a totally devoted apostle of he Most Precious Blood and of the Virgin. Those present at his death were convinced that Mary had appeared to him. He breathed serenely, looking up into the sky muttering: "O my Lady, my hope, my consolation."

Merlini justifiably enjoyed a reputation for holiness. At Sonnino, which he visited often, they called him the Saint. He was seen walking without an umbrella once under pouring rain as he rushed to bring the last rites to someone who was dying. He remained completely dry. In Rome he cured a blind woman. There was great excitement at his healing the sight of a certain

Rori in Sonnino. He cured others during the Rome cholera epidemic in 1867. He could read into the recesses of one's conscience and was able to predict events which occurred as he had foretold them. Even after his death, up to our own day, many have claimed to have received grace through his intercession. A number of these claims have been meticulously investigated and have been found to be authentic.

In 1972 the Church officially recognized the heroic nature of the virtue that he exercised. There were many souls that wished him to be canonized so that they might venerate him alongside St. Gaspar and the Blessed Maria De Mattias.

A LUMINOUS CONSTELLATION. To the most illustrious, others, no less illustrious in doctrine and holiness must be added. Among these: Bishop Guglielmo Sillani–Aretini, who left the Bishopric of Terracina to follow St. Gaspar. Possessed of a large and generous heart, he was known as the angel of charity. He was a very learned man. He has left us a biography (unfortunately incomplete) of the Founder and the history of the Annals of the Early Years of the Congregation. We recall *Don* Vincenzo De Nicola a man of elevated habits and the consoling angel of whomever was afflicted by need and pain. We bring to mind also Don Innocenzo Betti, the apostle of Benevento. During a course of Spiritual Exercises at St. Felix, he revealed to the Saint that he had been thinking of becoming a Capuchin. But when later on he complained about having been given a narrow room with a little window, Gaspar said to him smiling: You see, you weren't meant to be a Capuchin. Stay with us and become a missionary." He had a number of disagreements with the Saint regarding the habit which the lay assistants wore, but then he bowed his head in obedience. He distinguished himself through his doctrine and his virtue.

Worthy of being remembered, finally, is Brother Giosafat Petrocchi of St. Elpidio delle Marche, who entered the Congregation late in life. He had been married and had children. He was very virtuous and when his wife died, he had dedicated himself totally to his parish, teaching catechism to the children and going among the homes to recite the rosary and dispense words of wisdom. He was a man of much charity. Upon learning of the reputation for sainthood which Gaspar enjoyed,

O. Scarpè

he went to St. Felix and entreated the Founder to take him in as a servant. His virtue and his apostolic ardour soon became apparent among the peasants of the countryside around St. Felix. He died leaving many who mourned his passing. Of him two things in particular were to be repeated; that he had done a great deal of good and that he had seen the angels descending from heaven on the Holy House of Loreto.

We regret that we cannot even include a list of the other countless companions who followed Gaspar in the early years of the apostolate and immediately after his death. We know how scrupulous and meticulous he was in his choice, for he wanted his companions to possess exceptional virtue and knowledge. And, even if some were not particularly suited to preaching, he wanted them at least to be desirous of hearing confession and of serving the Church and upholding her decorum. Above all he wanted men of prayer. They made up a veritable luminous constellation of generous and holy souls through whom "It has pleased God to bless our Congregation from the very beginning, almost as if to confer on it, through the magnificence of their virtues, the seal of his sovereign approbation."

Maria De Mattias, listening to a sermon of Gaspar, receives the call to a religious vocation and on his advice founds the Institute of the Adoring Sisters of the Blood of Christ.

After the consecration he sees chains of gold coming from the chalice to envelop his soul.

O. Scarpelli

THE MISSIONS
BRIGANDAGE
MARIA DE MATTIAS

An obstinate sinner on the verge of death refuses the Sacraments. Gaspar scourges himself until he obtains his conversion.

THE MISSIONS

Having opened the first House, Gaspar returned to Rome in search of priests interested in preaching at the Missions. For him, the missionary spirit was synonymous with the spirit of the priesthood and the spreading of devotion to the Most Precious Blood.

While following the example of the great missionary saints of the past, his method was all his own, bearing, as it did, the stamp of his doctrine, his piety and his charity. There are still extant a few copies of the Method for the Holy Missions which Gaspar had printed.

He did not accept Missions unless they were requested by the local authorities or approved by them. He would choose proselytizers most suited and best equipped for the places they would be operating in. He insisted that they make their entrance into the area with great solemnity. The Missionaries had to be received by the clergy, by the local authorities and by the populace amidst sacred hymns and the pealing of bells. It was not out of a sense of "triumphalism" that he required all of this, but that he wanted to make everyone aware that it was "a moment of the manifestation of God's mercy". When he arrived, he would prostrate himself and kiss the ground. The Crucifix would be brought to him and then they would proceed into the church. The inaugural sermon would start immediately and as he spoke the preacher would flagellate himself. Sometimes they would all go immediately to the platform, put on a crown of thorns and scourge themselves. These acts were not mere ostentation. This initial "ritual" was meant to set the tone for the entire duration of the Mission and to bring all of the people into the church. The Mission generally lasted about fifteen days, during which the Missionaries spiritually assailed the populace without respite. Shops, cafes and bars were to remain closed. Usually there were four sermons a day: two in the morning, with catechism on the Decalogue, and the examples from the life of the Virgin Mary, whose image, known as Our Lady of the Most Precious Blood was exhibited on an altar or on a stage; two in the evening, with an instruction on the sacrament of Confession and the main sermon on the Four Last Things (Death, Judgement, Heaven, Hell). During the fifteen days there were also specific lectures given to the various strata of society: the clergy, professionals, mothers, fathers, youth and children. The evening events were reserved for men only. One day was set aside during which the sick and those in prison were visited and brought Holy Communion in a solemn ceremony. Great importance was given to the procession of penitence with the Dead Christ during which all the people who took part wore a crown of thorns and scourged themselves along with the Missionaries. The number of arms, obscene prints, playing cards, cult objects, and emblems of sects collected was enormous and the entire pile was burned in a public bonfire. Good books and sacred images were widely distributed.

It is easy to understand how tiring those days of proselytizing were. The only period of rest during the day was lunch time, at which however, no talking was allowed. Instead, there were readings from some sacred text or the life of a saint.

The main reason for having a Mission was to convert sinners. God always blessed the work of the Missionaries and of Gaspar in particular because the crowds at the confessionals were large. Obviously Gaspar's confessional was "assailed" more than the others. "He had such an effective way of attracting and receiving the penitent and of getting them to repent that no one ever left him without being truly converted and totally happy." As to his method of confessing, it was, Merlini says: "Patient, prudent and benign, these were the skills he brought to the confessional which he was also to counsel others to use." And he adds: "He was an excellent director of souls, and he guided my spirit also." It is well–known that many were guided by him and people from all walks of life came to him, including prelates, nobles and cardinals. He was the spiritual director of various religious communities, both male and female.

During the Missions, Gaspar would establish Pious Works which would perpetuate the fruits of their labours: the Retreat of the Twelve Apostles for the Clergy, the Sisters of Charity, the Daughters of Mary, the Luigini, the Retreat of the Peasants, prayer Groups, the Oratory of St. Francis Xavier with its own Retreat, the Pious Union of the Most Precious Blood whose purpose was the Perpetual Adoration and of the solemn celebration of the Feast of the Month of the Most Precious Blood. Most moving was the ceremony of the *Seven Effusions* with prayers, lectures and songs in honour of the Blood of Christ. Very effective for the conversion of the more obstinate sinners, was the sudden entrance of the image the Sorrowful Virgin through the main doors of the church, amidst weeping and shouts of "Hail Mary", the playing of the organ and the pealing of bells.

Unforgettable was the day of reconciliation. During the sermon in church or in the open, the most unyielding of enemies would make peace and age–old hatreds would come to an end. Family would embrace family in public and entire villages in the surrounding countryside would meet to make peace. The bells would peal festively, those present would be spurred on to participate, hymns would be sung and prayers recited in unison. We would like to point out here that it was St. Gaspar who initiated the custom in many towns of ringing the bells at vespers to recall the Passion of Jesus and after the Angelus in the evening in memory of the departed.

At the end of the Mission, in an open place, a *Memorial Cross* would be raised. The crosses raised by the Saint are still preserved in many of these towns.

The Missionaries, after having done so much good, would leave in secrecy in order to avoid any festivities in their honour. There was to be honour and glory only to God. However, on

O. Scarpelli

many occasions the people had learned of the time of their departure nd often would shut the city gates or block the roads in order to have them remain one more day.

THE APOSTLE

Except for a brief period in 1826 when the Pope assigned him to work for the "Propaganda Fide", from 1815, the year of the birth of the Congregation, until his death (December 28, 1837) Gaspar dedicated himself to preaching Missions of conversion. The number of the Houses of the Institute kept growing as did the number of priests and the lay brothers that became part of it. Besides the one at St. Felix, houses were opened during the life of Gaspar at Pievetorina, Albano, Terracina, Sonnino, Sermoneta, Velletri, Frosinone, Vallecorsa, Benevento, Rimini, Nepi, Cesena, Macerata, Feltria and Pennabilli. The requests for Missions were many. On the one hand Gaspar rejoiced at this; on the other he suffered because he was unable to satisfy everyone. He was more concerned, and justly so, with the quality of the priests than with their numbers when he considered whether or not to accept them into the Institute. Like a well armed detachment, Gaspar and his Missionaries would take off from these Houses to fight the evils of society and the anarchical and atheistic Sects; they would go with love among the people who because of poverty and ignorance brought about by wars and injustice, had forgotten God and embarked on a life of vice. The field of the apostolate was vast and it is impossible here to list even only a few of the numerous places which Gaspar visited in Lazio, Umbria, Marche, Romagna, Abruzzo and the Kingdom of Naples. His method was always the same wherever he went. Still, every Mission was distinguished from every other by some particular thing which was its very own.

After the founding of the Institute, Gaspar began his apostolic journey at Benevento. Let us listen to what the Apostolic

A sectarian who had set out to stab him to death, once he finds himself in Gaspar's presence, feels the knife falling from his hand.

77

Legate to the city had to say in a letter. "I have been sent into a forest full of wild beasts rather than reasonable men...a rabble without legitimate birth, without manners, without education. It is truly a miracle if at any moment an uprising does not occur!" In fact the Missionaries were forced to enter the city by night because it was feared that there would be a popular movement against them. Before the arrival of the Missionaries, the city had been covered with blasphemous posters ridiculing the Eucharist, the Virginity of Mary, and the principal Truths of the Faith and while inciting the people to rise up against the Pope. Within fifteen days, the city was completely transformed. Public retractions took place; a group of students who before had been bitter enemies and detractors, now wanted to carry the Missionaries about in triumph. Gaspar undertook the most difficult and demanding work and was the most convincing. After the Mission the Apostolic Legate wrote: "There is no more swearing...The whole city is full of compunction." A few persuasive sermons had been more effective than troops. The fame of the Missionaries had spread all the way to Naples, where many great sinners came from to confess to the Fathers.

The Memorial Cross which Gaspar erected in the Square of the Duomo is still intact after the bombings of the Second World War, even though the Duomo itself was razed to the ground.

Immediately after this Mission at Benevento, Pius VII, after seeing the great good achieved by the Missionaries, sent Gaspar and the same priests to preach another mission at Frosinone. They arrived at night, after a very arduous journey. They were given a very warm reception full of affection by the clergy and the people who had been waiting for them. The streets were lit up and the preaching began. This Mission, also, bore much fruit. "The quantity of arms," wrote Guglielmi, a leading citizen, "which the greatest scoundrels brought to the feet of the Our Lady was infinite!" In a large banner spanning the street they had written: "Don Gaspar, you have stolen our hearts!" From then on he would direct all the Missions in which he took part and they would be, by and large, organized by the Missionaries of the Most Precious Blood.

We shall now take, as it were, a bird's eye view of the long and arduous missionary journey of Gaspar, naming only a few of the places he visited.

Without ever neglecting Rome and the works of charity he had initiated there and while making sure that the churches of the various Houses of the Congregation were kept running efficiently and that the Spiritual Exercises for Nuns and Priests were kept up, he preached at Holy Missions and in various localities.

1816 at Frosinone, Civitavecchia and Rieti where a white dove was seen circling his head while he was preaching and, during the sermon on the Last Judgement, a flash of lightning traversed the church from one window to the other even though the sky was clear.

The most renowned Mission was at Ancona, "stronghold of the enemies of the Pope and Religion", where the sectarians incited the people against the Missionaries to the point of threatening their lives. Instead the people answered by being converted in droves, burning blasphemous prints and taking part in a General Communion which "seemed never to end".

After Ancona he went to Bagnaia and then to Porto d'Anzio, where he spent time ministering to the inmates of various penal institutions. From there he went to Ardea, to Pratica di Mare and then to Velletri.

In 1817 he was at Cisterna where among the people of the Marshlands, every kind of crime was rife and the scourge of malaria assailed the region. Here he instituted the "Confraternity of the Good Death" for the christian and civil burial of those who died of malaria, who had up to then been thrown like carrion into the bog. During the sermon at Cisterna, he stopped the heavy rainfall by reciting a Hail Mary. In April, after Civitavecchia, he went to Cori, where, by scourging himself he succeeded in bringing peace to the people who were divided into two factions which often engaged in armed clashes resulting in death and injury. Then he went to Sermonetta where during his sermon on death, he invited all those present to receive God's grace and said: "Who can say whether some of you will be here to listen to God's voice tomorrow!"

The following evening a certain Pasquale Tomarosi lay in his casket in the middle of the church. One can imagine how many confessions took place! At Loreto he won over a holy Priest to

the Congregation, Don Biagio Valentini, whom we have already mentioned briefly and who was cured of tuberculosis by Gaspar. He went to Montefano in Macerata and from there to Civitanova Marche where the episode narrated by Valentini, who was an eye witness, took place. A very pretty woman, but lascivious and a breeder of scandal, tried to dissuade people from going to listen to the words of Gaspar by making fun of him. She died suddenly and her body was found horribly transformed. This episode produced a general feeling of salutary horror and was cause for many conversions. It also greatly increased his fame of holiness. In November he went to Rome, Roccamassima and Giulianello nel Lazio.

1818 – This year was dedicated almost entirely to the Regions Marche and Romagna. In fact, after the Mission at Nocera Umbra where in one day he delivered 16 sermons and calmed a violent storm, he went to Fabriano. Here, some men tried to corrupt him with gold coins. Refusing indignantly he answered them saying: "Souls, not gold!" His voice, though greatly weakened because of the stress of continual preaching, was heard many miles away. He went immediately to Matelica, where he struggled vehemently against Masonic and Carbonari Sects. In this little city there also occurred two prodigious events.

During the sermon, a luminous sphere hovered over Gaspar's head and the Silvestrine monk, Don Gregorio Ambrosi, heard the voice of Gaspar, who was preaching a quarter of a mile away. In going to Colleamato, his horse slipped and remained with his rear legs miraculously suspended over the abyss. From there he went to St. Severino Marche and then to St. Elpidio a Mare and then again to Ancona. The Missions at Forlimpopoli and Meldola in Romagna were very famous and are still remembered. In these little towns, the Sectarians ruled. Though he received a number of death threats, he succeeded with his words and his deeds in converting a large number of the citizens and in

Gaspar refuses to reveal the secrets of the confessional to a nobleman, who fires at him at point blank range. The bullet falls harmlessly at the feet of Gaspar.

winning over the hearts of the people. The Sectarians handed over their arms and their cult symbols in droves. At Forlimpopoli a few wayward young men went to live it up in a small villa far from the town so as not to hear his sermon. Instead, they heard his voice as clearly as if they were in the square of the town.

An executioner who had gone expressly to kill him, once he came into his presence, saw the knife falling out of his hand and he knelt before him and asked for forgiveness. At Meldola they gave him poison, but he blessed the potion and drank it without harm. At Meldola, also, occurred the miracle of bilocation. Many people saw him preaching on the platform in the square at the same time as he was in the confessional. So great was the crowd which flocked to see him that many climbed up to the roofs and the tops of trees that were in the square. After his long stay in Romagna he went to the following towns in the Marche: Castelfidardo, Montelupone, Montecassiano and Cerreto, Serra St. Quirico, Sassoferrato and Gualdo Tadino. At Cerreto, also, the miracle was repeated of his voice being heard a few miles from where he was preaching. Another wonder occurred at the Mission while he was preaching at Serra St. Quirico. Don Biagio Valentini received a letter begging him to go immediately to his mother's side since she was dying. Gaspar exhorted him not abandon the good work he was doing among the faithful, assuring him that the Lord would provide. Valentini obeyed. The Mission had not yet come to an end when the sad news arrived. His mother had died happily, with her missionary son by her side. The miracle of simultaneity had occurred, due to the heroic act of obedience performed by Don Biagio.

1819 – In this year full of sorrow for Gaspar, he went on a Mission to Pievetorina where he had the choice dishes which had been offered to the Missionaries distributed to the poor. From there he went to Caldarola and, during the sermon, he calmed a violent storm by blessing the heavens; he also healed a gravely ill person, giving him ham to eat which he had blessed. Here he cured Maria Cecchina who was mentally ill and the man from Pieve, a certain Massi, who was also seriously ill.

At St. Ginesio he converted in extremis a priest who had long before abandoned the church and refused the Sacraments. He moved him to repent by scourging himself: "I will beat myself for your sins and will not stop until the Grace of God triumphs!" The Missions at St. Anatolia, Apiro and Camerino followed, where Gaspar was subjected to public vilification, but the people came in such numbers to fill the square that "a grain of millet could not be squeezed in". Firearms, prints, amulets and other similar objects were destroyed. From July to December Gaspar and his followers were at Sarnano, at Comachio and in various other surrounding towns. Thence he went into the dioceses of Rimini and preached Missions at Canonica, St. Arcangelo, Savignano and St. Giovanni in Marignano. At Canonica he cured Don Giuseppe Maggioli who was on the point of death. From Romagna at Moscosi he went to the Marche, to Belforte and other nearby towns. Requests for Missions came to Gaspar from many places and he was pained at having to refuse many of them. He would repeat with sadness: "How can we possibly make everyone happy?"

Mons. Albertini, who in April 1819 had been consecrated Bishop of Terracina, invited him to conduct a Mission in this city. Gaspar went there in November and achieved a resounding success. The holy bishop himself wrote: "The crowds at the confessionals are immense; suffice it to say that they went so far as to stay up all night waiting in front of the church so they could confess in the morning." But this happiness was not to last long. Immediately after this Mission, the holy Bishop died of malaria. Gaspar lost the spiritual father who had guided him for so many years and who held him more dear than a son. His anguish was great. The Pope proposed Gaspar to succeed him in running that Dioceses, but, in all humility, he refused. Mons. Carlo Manasse, auxiliary missionary of the Most Precious Blood, was appointed to the post.

1820 – Mons. Vincenzo Strambi called Gaspar "a spiritual earthquake" because of his habit of never resting or pausing during his sermons. The year began with the great Mission at Velletri. The populace was in a state of agitation because of a particularly bloody fratricide. The feelings of hatred were running high and even among the confraternities there often arose bitter disputes. The Bishop, Cardinal Alessandro Mattei also happened to die while the Mission was going on. It took all

of Gaspar's diplomatic skills and fervour in so delicate a situation to bring peace to those souls so incensed by hatred. God helped him and here, too, the Mission ended with complete success. During a sermon in the square all those who had been enemies embraced each other, and that embrace marked the beginning of a lasting peace.

Velletri was followed by the Mission at Fabbrica di Roma, after which he went to Spello a small city in Umbria which has remained famous for the many and prodigious works and the many fruits of his preaching. In this town there was the custom of paying for the amount of wax used after the sacred functions and the processions were over. How great was the surprise of the merchants, Feliciano Angelini, Lorenzo Merello and Giovanni Bellucci in observing, after a long service, followed by a procession during which the candles had been burning continuously, that on weighing the wax again at the end, instead of diminishing, the weight had actually increased! The episode is recounted by Merlini, who was a witness to it. It also happened that during a sermon in the square a luminous cross made up of tiny stars was seen shining over the head of Gaspar.

Having gone to the nearby Fiammenga, Gaspar began traversing the countryside with a large cross inviting all the people he met to come to the functions. One evening, while he was preaching in the square, "a very bright light" descended from the sky and shone on the painting of the Queen of the Most Precious Blood whence it was reflected for a long time onto the face of Gaspar. During this Mission he cured an invalid who "had been given up for lost" by the doctors, by making the sign of the cross over him with the image of St. Francis Xavier. Gaspar, as can be seen from written documents and recorded eye–witness accounts, enjoyed "an exceptional state of spiritual elevation" during this period. He attributed everything to the Most Precious Blood, the Virgin and St. Francis Xavier.

After a period of Spiritual Exercises at St. Felix, where the

The miracle of bitocetion (simultaneous presence in two diffenent places); he is seen preaching in the square at the same time as he is seen in the confessional in the church.

first meeting between Gaspar and the Venerable Merlini took place, Gaspar was at Torricchio and Mergo. Here, just after he had begun his sermon on the Last Judgement, the same thing happened which had occurred at Spello. "A very bright star, with three points, hovered over his head during the whole sermon, and moved about as the holy Missionary moved." On his way back to St. Felix he cured a young boy who had severely injured his knee and who, according to the doctors, would be crippled for life.

He continued his journeys through Umbria and after Terzo della Pieve, he went to Grutti, near Todi, where he was acclaimed as the "Angel of God and bearer of peace", even by the clergy who had previously been sceptical about his holiness. He passed on to Cannara and thence he was to be found among the inmates of Rocca di Spoleto and at Origlio. After a stay in Rome where he had to attend to official business for the Congregation, he went on a Mission to Subiaco in November. There, as in many other places, by blessing the heavens he brought an end to a heavy downpour which threatened to interrupt the open–air ceremonies. At Subiaco we encounter for the first time alongside Gaspar, the lay brother, Bartolomeo Panzini, who was to remain very faithful to Gaspar until his death. He was, however, quite arrogant and ill–tempered and liked to order everyone around. He was to be the "cross" which Gaspar would bear willingly all his life "to expiate his sins and to mortify himself", as he himself would say, encouraging everyone to look for the good in the uncouth fellow rather than the bad.

During this year Gaspar also held, for the second time, a Mission in Rome, at the Basilica of St. Nicola in Carcere, which bore much fruit and yielded many converts.

1821 – The feet of this great apostle could not keep still. The love of Christ propelled him towards those souls thirsting after God. He devoted almost the entire first half of this year to the Castelli Romani, covering also Marittima and Campagna, beginning at Ariccia, then going to Marino and thence to Castelgandolfo. It is no easy task to relate how much good was accomplished and how numerous were the manifestations of piety and the conversions in those little towns. At Castelgandolfo, while Gaspar was preaching in the crowded square, a farmer who had no liking for the faith or for priests wanted to walk though the crowd while pulling his loaded donkey behind him. The animal, wiser than its master, knelt and refused to go any further despite its owners blows and swearing. Only after the sermon was over did it get up and placidly go on its way. In February of that year, Gaspar and his followers went to Civita Lavinia and to Porto d'Anzio, where they cared for the inmates of the Darsena. Thence they went to Nettuno.

1821 was the joyous year of the opening of the House at Albano Laziale, which was to become one of the most famous places in the life of Gaspar and of his Congregation. After a solemn triduum to the Most Precious Blood, which Gaspar preached in the church of St. Paul, the Missionaries took possession of it. The rejoicing of the populace, who knew both Gaspar and his Brothers well, was immense. That day marked the beginning of a long journey along the path of good works, care, a saintly life and zeal towards the generous inhabitants of this area. The people were always to repay with affection and esteem the work of the Missionaries, affection and esteem which were to be perpetuated through time all the way down to our own day.

After opening this House, Gaspar covered the area around Viterbo and preached Missions at Barbaresco and at Bieda. From here he went to the Marche to hold a Mission at Chiaravalle, where people came in droves from the surrounding towns of Montemarciano, Monte St. Vito, Mosciano, Camerano, Castelferretti and Falconara. At Chiaravalle he subdued a hurricane so that the procession of the famous and prodigious Crucifix which is so venerated in this little city could take place. At Camerano a coach fell into a precipice and because of Gaspar's invocations no one was hurt. He went back to visit the Holy House at Loreto where, while at prayers, it was revealed to him how much suffering still lay ahead, "Crosses, crosses, always crosses!" Gaspar exclaimed with resignation as he came out of the church. On his way to Ascoli he passed through Montefalco where, while he celebrated mass on the altar of St. Chiara, he heard a voice confirming the revelation received at Loreto" "Prepare to suffer!" But had he not already suffered enough? No, he was still to do battle against the forces

O. Scarpelli

unleashed against him by the Enemy. God wanted his Servant to resemble Christ more and more.

He took off again on a Mission to Offida where a very ancient Relic of the Most Precious Blood was venerated and here he "had the opportunity to abandon himself along with the people to that ardour which burned in his heart for the Blood of Christ." Passing through Pievetorina, after visiting the Mother House at Giano, he went to preach a great Mission at Albano Laziale, whose memory will long endure in the minds of the people. The old people of Albano still recall that their grandparents told stories of large quantities of firearms being burned and many reconciliations taking place. Astounded at the great success of the Mission at Albano, they insisted on having him also in the nearby town of Genzano. Here a man "long inured to vice and sin refused to listen to the Missionaries and derided them". On the last night of the Mission he heard a priest preaching right below his window at the top of his voice to... no one. In fact there was no one in the deserted street. He reflected on this: " The Lord has come to seek me out at home, I really must return to Him." He received confession and communion while all looked on in amazement.

And how did Gaspar rest after so much work? He went to Rome and threw himself body and soul into the numerous works of charity which were so close to his heart.

BRIGANDAGE

Here we interrupt the year by year history of the apostolic life of Gaspar to relate how large a part he played in converting the brigands and in alleviating the sorrows of the people of southern Lazio. This Region was infested with faithless and heartless men who had fallen into a state of unimaginable brutishness and cruelty. Gaspar's work among them was truly of titanic proportions and would on its own be cause enough for his being

While preaching in the open, three very bright stars appear over his head.

remembered as one of the greatest Missionaries ever known and one of mankind's greatest benefactors. The zeal, the struggles, the calumny, the physical danger encountered and the results obtained would alone be sufficient to justify his canonization!

At first the phenomenon of brigandage could be attributed to the refusal of young men to be conscripted into the armies of Napoleon. With the fall of Napoleon, the phenomenon neither ended nor decreased. In fact, it became ever more widespread.

The complete descent into brutishness, due to living in the mountains and being isolated from civilized society, catapulted those men to committing a string of ever more heinous crimes. One might almost say that they hungered more after blood than money. Wherever they went, they left such a trail of slaughter as to instill terror into the bravest of hearts. Ensconced among the gorges and the caverns of the most inaccessible mountains of Ciociaria, they swooped down like hawks on the towns and roads below, where they pillaged and looted and left behind them corpses strewn about in their wake. To those who had deserted became allied those who were hardened criminals. Sonnino and Vallecorsa were the main strongholds of their impregnable fortresses with other centres at Carpineto, Gavignano, Bassiano, Sezze, Prossedi, Sermoneta and Patrica. The first massacre took place at Vallecorsa where ten people who had held public office under the Napoleonic government were slaughtered together on the night of Holy Thursday, 1814. Covered in ample cloaks under which they hid muskets and knives, the brigands entered the church of St. Martin and perpetrated their act of savagery among the faithful. To understand the brutality of this episode, suffice it to say that one woman was knifed to death on the altar of the Sepulchre, in the presence of Jesus in the Sacrament!

The brigands wore distinctive and picturesque clothing: velvet jackets, the so–called *devil's skin*, cone–shaped hats with wide brims, vests festooned with fluttering ribbons, knickers, clogs on their feet, pistols and large knives in their belts, unkempt beards and hair, a leather purse across their shoulder and a profusion of amulets, medals, coins and chains.

Each group had its own leader with power over life and death. The best known among them was Gasbarrone. Nothing was safe from them. The road from Rome to Naples was often the scene of their sudden ambushes. They stole everything and left behind the dead. Obviously their main targets were the rich, the nobles and the clergy. Their vendettas were punctual and ruthless.

It is impossible here to recount even a small part of their deeds. We will only allude to a few episodes which will give us an idea of their savagery and will help us to better understand the role played by Gaspar, apostle of peace amid such barbarism.

A necessary prerequisite for belonging to one of the bands was to have murdered someone. This led many misguided young men, fascinated by the stories of their deeds, to kill whoever might chance their way, simply to be able to join.

On the evening of May 23, 1821, the brigand chieftain, Massaroni, with a group of about twenty men burst into the Seminary at Terracina, in the convent of St. Francis. They took about thirty hostages, between seminarians and others. While they were dragging them away, a policeman came upon the scene and they shot him on the spot, killing the Vice–Principal, Don Domenico Cirillo, as well, for having gone up to the officer of the law to administer the last rites. The prisoners tried to take advantage of the confusion and attempted to escape but only about ten of them succeeded. The rest, a number of wounded among them, were recaptured and taken into the mountains. Massaroni sent two of them to warn the relatives and the authorities that the hostages would not be released unless they paid a huge ransom.

Since it was impossible to pay such an enormous sum, the people tried to win over the criminals by sending large quantities of food into the mountains. The brigands held firm. Collections were taken, the Bishop donated his gold pectoral cross, families and friends gave their valuables. Only when they had received forty thousand *scudi* did the brigands let everyone go, except for two who had been slaughtered near the Caves of Monte S. Biagio.

Another such episode was the audacious assault on the hermitage of Tuscolo near Frascati where all the Camaldolesi hermits were captured. The monks were gathered in prayer when they were attacked, tied up and forcibly led away. The

O. Scarpel

brigands, with Vittori leading them, left behind a one hundred year old friar who was told that if they didn't receive seventy thousand scudi within three days, they would massacre all of his brothers. The Monks were dragged through the forests of Faiola and Molara and into the territory of Artena. Then the brigands took the hostages to Roccamassima. The poor friars tried to convince their malefactors that the sum they demanded was so exorbitant, that they would not have been able to raise it even if they sold the hermitage.

A large detachment of police was despatched. The bandits were attacked in force and forced to flee again with the hostages. They reached their stronghold at Monte St. Biagio and from there they sent Don Ubaldo Ceccarelli with a demand that he bring the ransom to Fossanova. The unfortunate incident had a happy ending near Sonnino, where, after a shoot–out with the police, the bandits fled, leaving their hostages free. Only one of them was seriously wounded.

Sonnino welcomed the monks to the festive pealing of bells.

Main highways, country roads, squares and towns were daily strewn with corpses and the severed heads belonging both to unarmed citizens and captured bandits. The Papal Government responded without mercy and even resorted to summary executions. The brigands captured and murdered; the authorities did likewise. The law of retaliation prevailed so that it was not uncommon to see the hanging bodies of brigands, their heads impaled on pikes alongside the mutilated corpses of civilians and policemen. This method of dealing with the crimes hardened even further the bandits and led to horrifying acts of vengeance. Mothers pointed out this slaughter to their children and made them swear an oath of vengeance. On occasion the Government would declare an amnesty, promising impunity to those who gave themselves up. But the promises were almost never kept and every one ended up on the gallows. Then the brigands, infuriated even further at the betrayal, intensified their

At Veroli a woman touches the hem of his cassock and her haemorrhaging is cured, as happened with the woman in the gospel.

raids and their slaughter.

Some of the brigands had the audacity to operate within reach of the walls of the city so that the populace of Rome and the Roman State were terrorized. The Pope, discouraged by all this, decided to take extreme measures and ordered that Sonnino, also known as brigandopolis, be razed to the ground.

At this juncture, Gaspar intervened. He alone had grasped the situation fully and faced head–on the anger of the Government and those whose vile interests led them to want the brigandage to continue. He defended Sonnino in a memorable and moving letter to the Pontiff which served to suspend the demolition which had already begun. For this reason, down to our own day, the Saint is revered as the father and saviour of the city.

We include a few passages from the famous letter of Gaspar to Pope Pius VII:

"Most Blessed Father!

Justice and mercy have always been the moving forces of all the works of Your Holiness. Even the demolition of Sonnino had justice as its motivation; and the demolition of the houses of the criminals has been justly carried out... But now that this initial demolition has been completed, it seemed that mercy would intervene. Justice may be brought to bear upon the guilty but not upon those who are not. So that this may not happen, the following reflections are submitted [for Your consideration]...

It would be ineffectual, since, coming as it does after the demolition of the houses of the guilty... the demolition of the other houses could not be of any consequence to them.

It would not become the exalted meekness of the Vicar of the God of peace if he proceeded inexorably toward the destruction of an entire town of three thousand souls and of its buildings, including sacred ones...

This demolition of an entire town and the dispersion of all its inhabitants would be fatal to agriculture...

It would be very dangerous for public safety to reduce such a large number of people to desparation; to leave hearth and home, relatives, possessions and one's own dwelling place leads to the greatest desolation...and if even a small part were to join the criminals...what might the consequences be?

Finally, if one justifies the demolition as a public measure and not as a punishment, then it would be unjust to destroy the property of the innocent without paying for the damages. If the damages are to be paid, then a million or at least half a million would not be sufficient to cover the costs. Given the present state of the treasury, such an expense could not be met...

In closing, may the clemency of Your Holiness cast its gaze on an entire populace who have only their eyes left to cry with."

The letter was so effective that the Pope became convinced that to redeem and call back the people from their state of barbarism to humanity and to God, only Religion and the energy of Gaspar Del Buffalo would work.

There was a great deal of evidence that pointed to the connivance of the authorities at all levels with the brigands. The police force of the Government was betrayed "by perfidious men". Some employees got rich from it and had honours heaped upon them. They were the "festering wound". "The Assembly of Delegates were a mass of villains." Gaspar, too, was profoundly saddened by this state of affairs. But he was not discouraged. Knowing full well whom he was up against, he began his undertaking at once. Along with Mons. Bellisario Cristaldi he prepared a plan for the elimination of the brigands from the Province of Marittima and Campagna, which was approved by Pius VII on October 8, 1821. The plan was based primarily on moral and religious principles which would certainly have served to render more amenable to civilized behaviour the inhabitants who were reduced to a state of "brutishness, barbarism and depravity".

To successfully coordinate his apostolic programme, Gaspar began by going through the difficult mountainous area of the Region where the brigands had taken on defensive positions as though they were at war, and he visited these villages in "Lower Lazio". He refused a police escort. The brigands were soon to be persuaded that he was a man of peace. He would only allow, even after much persistence, his faithful lay brother, Bartolomeo, to accompany him. He opened six Mission Houses in the most dangerous areas: Terracina, Sonnino, Sermoneta, Velletri, Vallecorsa, and Frosinone. He made a detailed report to the Bishops and to Rome making it quite clear that the people in the area were more eager than the Government itself to have

brigandage brought to an end. The Saint succeeded in penetrating the forest and the very caverns where the dangerous criminals were hiding out; his only weapon was a Crucifix. He spoke to them in a language of love which they had never heard before and he moved them so much that they threw themselves at his feet in an act of humble submission. He urged them to put their trust in the mercy and goodness of the Pope; he promised he would defend their cause if they put down their arms. He not only promised, but he kept his word by pleading with the authorities and the Holy Father to stop the repressive measures and the torturing of captured brigands. One day he encountered some policemen who had captured a bandit and had tied him across the back of a donkey like a sack: they were taking him around the countryside, pricking him with their bayonets to the cruel snickering and catcalls of the people who seemed to be enjoying the cruelty of the bloody spectacle.

By now the brigands had such faith in Gaspar that they followed him about in secret to ensure that he was safe from possible enemies. They also came in the dead of night to visit the Houses of the Mission whose doors were always open to them so that they could come in without having to wait. There they listened to the words of Gaspar or of some other Missionary and sang sacred hymns. This radical change in the behaviour of the brigands gave rise to a bitter battle against Gaspar by those whose interests had been affected. He was even accused of being in collusion with them against the State.

On November 20, 1821, after a solemn Mission, Gaspar opened the House at Terracina.

As was his custom, propelled by the great zeal which burned in his heart, he neglected his health; so much so that, in traversing back and forth over the Pontine Marshes he contracted malarial fever so serious that he was forced to return to Rome. He was so weak he could hardly stand and his face was like that of a corpse. He entreated Valentini to bless him with

Gaspar predicts to two Missionaries that they will soon die.

the relic of St. Francis Xavier and he immediately felt better. Even though he was so incapacitated, he set about putting the Institutes affairs in order and by the end of the year he preached a Mission at Segni. Valentini relates that a man there had sold his soul to the devil by signing a formal document, in exchange for a daily sum which the fiend would provide for him in a certain spot. However, the more money he received, the worse he felt and the more terrified he became. He had never before had the courage to confess this to anyone. He went to Gaspar who comforted him and gave him absolution and freed him from his nightmare. Valentini notes that the man's conversion was genuine and permanent.

1822 – We will now pick up again Gaspar's heroic, apostolic itinerary. In the middle of winter he went to Carpineto. His suffering continued to increase, because he too, like Christ, had a traitor in his midst: Don Giacomo Gabellini. He waged a campaign against him, sending a constant stream of letters to the enemies of Gaspar, even accusing him of being proud and inept. He was to cause a great deal of harm to the Institute with his scheming. Gaspar was forced to visit the various Houses to give heart to the Missionaries. He told them how happy he was with the good they were doing and that it was necessary to suffer a little in the cause of the Lord. They had to believe that evil would not triumph over good because in the end the truth would win out. Then he went to Anagni to make arrangements with the Bishop about opening a House in that populous little city. However, not only did this initiative come to naught, but he was also ill–treated by the Bishop's secretary. Evening had almost fallen and without even knowing the way, he set out with a fellow brother over the countryside covered with snow, heading towards Acuto. He began to talk to his companion of perfect happiness and, inspired by the moon–lit landscape, he glorified with him the immensity of God and they began singing praises to the Lord. From Acuto, where he conducted a Mission, he set out for Frosinone where he converted en masse an entire sect of Freemasons who brought along their insignias and burned them on the spot. He began negotiations for opening a Mission House there and then went, on March 3, to Vallecorsa, even though everyone tried to dissuade him from doing so because that town had the distinction of being the stronghold of the bloodiest of the brigand bands. It was here that he first came into contact with Maria De Mattias. Sillani writes the following of this Mission: "How great was the joy of the people at the sight of him as father and friend among them! With what devotion they received him, how moved they were in listening to his words from the platform!" The brigands had sewn much hatred amongst families in this land. Fathers had seen their children killed, children their fathers; the bride had lost her bridegroom, sisters their brothers. Ancient feuds and ancestral hatred were rampant and the cause of many crimes. Everyone wanted the Missionaries to make their home there in a Mission House. Merlini drew up plans for a House and a church and the foundations were quickly laid. The people vied with each other in carrying on their shoulders the stones and other building material for the construction. Of all those who helped, Maria De Mattias stood out among the crowd.

From Vallecorsa, Gaspar on foot as usual, went to hold a Mission at Norma di Piglio and then at Bassiano where they asked him to pass though an infertile olive grove and bless it. "From then on," wrote the parish priest "it always gave forth abundant fruit." He then went to Benevento to hold a second Mission. The people of Benevento remembered the benefits received from Gaspar during the famous Mission of 1815 and they welcomed him with great enthusiasm, thanking him for having built a Mission House in their city. The fruit of this Mission was no less abundant than that of the first and we leave with the reader the name of Don Innocenzo Betti, whom Gaspar left there to open the Mission House.

While Gaspar went far and wide, often at the expense of his health and sometimes with his very life in danger, spreading the Word of God with great zeal and redeeming for Him hordes of sinners, in Rome there were those who were plotting against him with anonymous letters and forged signatures. His life of martyrdom was never to cease until his death. It was not difficult for him to show, proof in hand, that the whole thing was an insidious fabrication and to track down the source of such accusations. He and his friends had renounced everything, even their own families and the comforts and peace of their own

homes. They had done this for the good of men's souls and to try to stamp out brigandage; how could they possibly deserve such calumny?

From Benevento he completed a round of Missions at Forlimpopoli and other localities in Romagna and finally he took a few days' rest at St. Felix. From here he wrote a long report to Cristaldi regarding the state of the Congregation. In it two things stand out: the holiness of the Missionaries and the good which they did. He also emphasised the poverty of the Mission Houses and the great joy of all the members of the Institute and the peace that pervaded among them amidst so many sacrifices. This is how he ends the report: "Jesus was born on a bed of straw and died on the cross. Now I have it in mind to do a tour of Provincia and of Campania and with God's help, I will do it on foot. We will save money this way!" In fact, he undertook the journey on December 19. He asked Merlini to come to Sezze for the Mission to be held there. Unknown to Gaspar, Merlini had been lying in bed for several days with malaria but he left immediately in any case. The Founder, seeing him in so weakened a state, took him to his room, blessed a cup of hot tea and gave it to him to drink. The following morning Merlini was feeling much better and took part in the various activities as though nothing had happened. On November 10, Gaspar held a Mission at Teramo which was so successful that the press talked about it for a long time. Gaspar himself said: "By the grace of the Most High, the Mission at Teramo has been one of the most glorious." Teramo was followed by the Missions at Campli, Civitella, Bellante, Montorio, Nereto, and Corropoli. It is practically impossible to relate how much work he did in all these places but we do not want to leave out one episode. On his way to Frontarola on foot, he was caught in a snow storm and did not arrive until night had fallen. Without even an umbrella to protect him and having had to climb the difficult 14 miles up the mountain side with nothing but his

Some members of a sect, in order not to listen to him, flee to live it up in the countryside, but the voice of Gaspar reaches them as though he were nearby.

biretta to cover his head, he arrived as white as a ghost on the evening of December 19. Once the word had spread that he had arrived, a large crowd gathered and he was forced to "preach" in that state.

Amidst great struggles, sacrifices, want and privation the Institute grew. What Gaspar often repeated with unshakeable faith was proving to be true: "The Missions are God's work. He will see to it that they flourish!"

1823 – Without neglecting his apostolic ministry, Gaspar dedicated a large part of that year to consolidating his Congregation. He was already making plans for a Boarding School in which young men could be trained for the missionary life. On February 12 the building of the House at Frosinone was begun. Gaspar, along with two companions, went off to preach a Mission at Priverno. Three of them were travelling with only one mount and one umbrella under a freezing downpour. They were soaked and covered in mud from head to toe when they arrived; still they began their Mission in the Cathedral without bothering to change. The people were moved merely by the sight of them and soon were soon won over by these pious Missionaries. The Mission was a complete success. Their enthusiasm reached its height when the people saw that, without an escort, the Missionaries had braved a journey up into the mountain carrying a large crucifix with them, in order to bring words of solace to the brigands. From there, Gaspar sent Don Giuseppe Marchetti to preach in nearby Maenza. When the latter had pointed out that he had never preached before in his life, Gaspar blessed him and reassured him. Don Giuseppe preached so well for the next eight days without assistance, that he won over the hearts of the people. When he spoke to Gaspar about it, Gaspar replied: "God always rewards obedience."

It may be useful to repeat here that in all of Gaspar's preaching, first and foremost he stressed devotion to the Most Precious Blood. He would say to everyone: "The Most Precious Blood of Jesus and the Virgin are the secret to obtaining an abundant harvest from the sacred Mysteries." On countless occasions he was acclaimed as the "Angel of peace" and whenever someone advised him to take some rest he would answer: "I shall rest in Heaven." After Priverno he went to

Veroli where he found a new Missionary, Don Vincenzo Fontana, who, as we have already seen, was a man of great virtue. "When he went to Prossedi," Santelli relates, "they were guests of Luigi Petoni Gabioli, who gave the Missionaries the worst wine in his well stocked cellars. Gaspar...took his revenge, as is befitting a Saint, by turning it into the best of his wines and ensuring that it lasted longer than any of the others he had." After three months of ministering to the Province of Lazio, he went to hold a Mission at Montalto near Offida.

Then he went to Ancona, where he dedicated himself with impressive results to ministering to those imprisoned for life in the penitentiary at Darsena. In September, with quite a few companions, he held a Mission at Pontecorvo in Lazio which lasted for fifteen days and "during which the prodigious events of the most famous Missions were repeated," according to one historian. There was a large number of conversions, peace was made between many feuding families and large quantities of arms and obscene prints were destroyed. A number of marvellous events also took place. By blessing those present with the Relic of St. Francis Xavier, over two hundred people were cured. He converted the leader of a Sect by inviting him to drink a glass of wine... When his fellow sectarians took him to task for having let the priest sway him, he answered: "I would like to have seen you there; in my position you would have done the same. You just can't say no to him." At the end of the year he went to Supino where, upon learning of the extreme poverty of many of the inhabitants, he set off through the snow with his haversack on his back and a bell in hand to knock on the doors of the rich. He was seen carrying away mattresses and other necessities and bringing them to the needy.

On August 23, 1823, to the great sorrow of Gaspar, Pope Pius VII died. With his death, Gaspar had lost a father, a benefactor and the protector of the Congregation. He ordered masses to be said for his soul in all the Churches of the Congregation. Cardinal Della Genga was elected as his successor under the name of Pope Leo XII. As we shall see, this Pope was to play a large role in the life of Gaspar.

1824 – Gaspar suffered from many ailments and he was much worn down by work and other sorrows. Nonetheless, at the

beginning of this year he evangelized in the Diocese of Gaeta, where the brigand, fra Diavolo roamed free to commit his bloody deeds. Then on to Fondi, Itri, Mola di Gaeta, Lenola, Castellone (modern day Formia) and Civita. At Itri a young man, while he was confessing, noticed that Gaspar was not listening to him because he was rapt in ecstasy.

Others that were waiting their turn, seeing that he was taking so long, pulled at his jacket. Gaspar awoke from his revery. "What a pity," the young man said. "It was so beautiful to look at his face all aglow and his eyes turned towards heaven!" Here too, there occurred yet again the phenomenon of his piercing voice returning after saying a prayer.

After completing the Mission at Guarcino he headed toward Sora where he was to conduct the Exercises with the Sacconi. Near Casamari he had a bad fall from his horse and the bolting animal dragged him along the road for quite a distance, but he was not even scratched in the incident.

During a sermon of the Mission at Guarcino two age–old enemies embraced in public in the church. The Missions preached by Gaspar's companions at Ventotene and Ponza were very difficult but fruitful and filled with memorable episodes. The Missionaries were housed in the cells of the Fortress! A priest who had not been to confession in forty years was converted. A tempest was becalmed. A certain individual who had sold his soul to the devil was freed by one of the missionaries who, however, was to suffer the effects of the Enemy's venge-ance. He became so ill that he almost died.

When he got back to Frosinone, he discovered that things were not going very well for him in Rome. There had been rumours of his death. At Teramo all the pious associations and the congregations founded by Gaspar were disbanded, even that of the little Louis. They were accused of being "Congreghe filled with the evil–minded, sectarians and drunkards." The

For a procession of the Dead Christ, there was no money to buy candles. Gaspar obtained the candles by agreeing to pay after-ward for the wax used. Amazingly, after so many hours, the wax weighed more than it had originally.

Bishop, who was ill–informed, ordered that the crucifix and the holy images be removed from their headquarters. It was open war against Gaspar. However, he never uttered one word of complaint. He would always say: "Let us humble ourselves before the Lord! An apostle needs a great deal of patience." They went so far as to accuse him of being the author of defamatory pamphlets and of having spoken out against his own missionaries at the Holy Congregation. Clearly these were all slanderous accusations born of hatred. With his usual inner strength all he said on the matter was: "To suffer, pray and remain silent – this is my motto."

At the beginning of September he went to preach a Mission at Campoli Appennino. This little town in Frusina was one of Gaspar's favourites. He performed many marvels there, as we shall see. He is still much venerated there today and it was here, after his death, he performed one of the miracles approved for his canonization.

This was also the year in which the first Boarding School of the Institute was opened at St. Felix at Giano. In September he organized Missions in the Dioceses of Penne and Atri. Another blow was to befall Gaspar. When he got to Giulianova, he found that he and all his Missionaries had been forbidden from cele-brating mass, preaching and hearing confessions in the entire Diocese. The Lord comforted and gave a sign of his goodness through the working of a miracle. The coach that was carrying the Missionaries went off the road and the wheels on one side remained suspended in mid–air over a deep chasm. It was a miracle that the horses did not bolt but remained motionless while the Missionaries got out and pulled the vehicle back onto the road. They had to proceed the rest of the way to Penne on foot under a heavy rain and arrived caked with mud. They had no water to wash with and had to use a bottle of white wine which had been given to them as a gift for this purpose. Word of the episode with the coach spread throughout the city and the inhabitants received them in triumph, joyous at news of the danger which had been averted. They became so attached to them that after the wonderful Mission which followed, they did not want them to leave.

After Penne, Loreto Aprutino had the great joy of receiving

the Missionaries. Gaspar in a letter blessed the Lord for the crowd which rushed up to the confessional. Then the Mission at Civita St. Angelo and Atri followed. Here, as Canon Don Nicola Palma relates, Gaspar took upon himself all of the apostolic work, despite serious swelling to his gums which forced him to drink only liquids. The townspeople were so grateful for his dedication and so moved that they would not hear of having him leave. He had to resort to disguising himself in order get away. He ended 1824 with the Mission at Pofi where "many books were burned and large quantities of arms were destroyed". At the end of this year Gaspar was overjoyed in being able to write: " There has not been up to now one Mission which, because of the merits of the Most Precious Blood, has not been accompanied by celestial gifts."

MARIA DE MATTIAS

Fifteen years had now passed since his exile, when Gaspar had learned of the prophecy of Sister Agnese of the Word Incarnate and he thanked God because, for the good of so many souls, that prophecy was coming to pass. He had for some time now been dreaming that an order of the Sisters of the Blood of Christ would soon become a reality. From the time he was a young man he had been working and continued still to work for the physical, moral and spiritual salvation of the young. Santa Galla was proof of his zeal and his success. And what of the young women? In the Missions, as a harbinger of Catholic Action, as John XXIII was to call him, he created institutions for every category and class of person so that good would continue to be done. How many young people fell victim to the vices of adults and to those of their very families? How many of them directly involved from a tender age in vice and schooled by ignorance became inured to these two plagues of humanity and ended up in the prisons! How many of them were being trained to be the criminals of tomorrow! He wanted to entrust them to the care of pious women in order that through their heroic acts of charity, these young children of the people could be re-deemed.

In prison he had written, along with Albertini, a Rule for the

O. Scarpelli

Sisters of the Most Precious Blood, consisting of twenty three articles. This Rule was to have been used by the marquise Caterina Bentivoglio who was to have been the Founder. But it was not she whom God had chosen. It was the will of Providence that this flower was to bloom right there, at Vallecorsa, where the bloodthirsty brigands flourished more than anywhere else.

In 1822, as we know, Gaspar went to preach a Mission in that little town in Ciociaria. Near the platform, a few metres from him, a young maiden was listening to him in ecstasy. He fixed her with his penetrating stare and showed her the Crucifix, as though to invite her to consecrate herself to Him in the name of His Blood. Had Gaspar, then, mysteriously sensed that she was the one God had designated to found the female branch of his Institute? When the Mission was over, Gaspar left; the soul of the maiden was troubled by uncertainty regarding her vocation. She intended to enter a monastery where strict enclosure prevailed. However, Gaspar's invitation to undertake the life of an apostle in the name of the Blood of the Crucified Christ seemed very clear. In the meantime she had time to reflect, and above all, to pray.

When Gaspar went back to Vallecorsa to inaugurate the new Mission House, she came to him for advice. Finally she received a clear and precise explanation for that penetrating stare and for his having singled her out with the Crucifix. "God is calling upon you to become a saint by living among the people and teaching the young." He urged her to seek the advice of a pious and learned person to assure herself that she should not make a mistake in the life she was to undertake. Maria went to the Santuario della Civita near Gaeta, and sought the guidance of a renowned Servant of God, Don Giuseppe Addessi. Merlini relates that the priest told her everything that was troubling her before she began to speak and exhorted her follow Gaspar's counsel.

In 1824 Gaspar sent Don Giovanni Merlini to preach at Vallecorsa and Maria chose him as her spiritual director and told

Gaspar, along with his horse, fell down a steep embankment. Miraculously, both he and the animal escaped unharmed.

him of a vision she had had during prayers: a crowd of Nuns and a voice "These are your companions". Gaspar intervened and told Merlini to continue guiding that soul who had been chosen by the Lord to achieve great things. He should do this both verbally and in writing because she was the woman predestined to be the Founder of the Sister Adorers of the Most Precious Blood of Jesus.

Gaspar would not personally be responsible for the Sisters because, since he was so persecuted he thought that they might become a target of the ruthless enemies of goodness.

After the death of her mother and her sister, Maria had to overcome the difficulties which her family raised and the affection which she felt toward her ageing father. Finally everyone gave in. Maria, on the advice of Merlini, asked the Bishop of Ferentino to send her to Acuto. She was enthusiastically received and explained to the Bishop and to the people that she had come not only to teach, but to found a Monastery of Nuns under the banner of the Most Precious Blood. And so, on March 4, 1834, with God's benediction, the new Institute of the Sister Adorers of the Blood of Christ was born. Twelve years had passed since the first meeting of Maria De Mattias and Gaspar. The way of God is long, but certain. Even if Gaspar did not personally direct it, he followed closely the fortunes of the Institute of the Adorers, and, through Merlini, helped establish its program, its objects, and the habit to be worn. He also gave Merlini the main outlines of the Rule.

The path traversed by this angelic creature and her developing Institute, despite many sacrifices and enormous hardships, was to be luminous and filled with marvels. Its goal, second only to the principal one of the Perpetual Adoration of the Blood of Christ, was the education and moulding of the young and the performing of acts of charity through various social institutions, such as hospitals, orphanages and rest homes. Maria soon distinguished herself through her ability, her prudence and her heroic virtues; everywhere she went her sanctity and her charity were infectious. She had the satisfaction of seeing her work spread throughout Italy. She also performed many marvels while she was alive. She died in Rome on July 20, 1866, with the Venerable Merlini at her side, singing the praises of the Most

Precious Blood. Merlini did not recite the De Profundis; he intoned rather the Te Deum.

After a number of miracles and intercessions, Pius XII beatified her in the Holy Year of 1950.

Today this worthy Institute has spread throughout the world and produces many good works, even in Foreign Missions. Although the requirements of the times have made some changes necessary to the dress code along with minor modifications to the Rule and way of life, the spirit of Gaspar, Merlini and of the Blessed Maria De Mattias has remained intact.

THE END OF THE BRIGANDS

After this moving digression dedicated to Maria De Mattias, we must return briefly to the history of brigandage. We must stress that, although Gaspar was able, with the help of his companions, to eradicate this evil, he was still to suffer many bitter disappointments. If we examine the conduct of Gaspar, we see that he was very brave, loyal and full of love for the outlaws whom he so desired to lead back to Christ.

The new pope Leo XII, wanted the definitive and absolute eradication of this plague. He approved of Gaspar's methods, realizing that it was much more effective to use humane and peaceful means and the strength of religion and moral persuasion, than to bring violent repression to bear on the situation. Merlini writes: "In the beginning we travelled cautiously accompanied by soldiers. Then we started moving about without them. Then, seeing that the bandits left us alone and would even hide when they saw us to avoid frightening us, as they told us later, we moved about with greater freedom." When Cardinal Consalvi forced the Missionaries to close the Houses built in the areas most frequented by the brigands because he was afraid there would be attacks on them, Gaspar pleaded with him to have them reopened. He wrote: "The brigands have seen us a hundred, a thousand times and they have also seen me and have left us in peace, even though they have often said that we are spies for the Government."

The Governor of Vallecorsa said that now the brigands were

the least of his worries whereas before the arrival of the Mission aries they could not keep track of all the murders. However, no one can have known the heroism, the privations and the moral and physical suffering of the Missionaries in those Houses. "Gaspar was always first into the fray, hurrying about, aglow with sublime charity, spurring on his brothers to have courage, to keep up the faith, to make one more sacrifice; he urged them to stay on where the air was unhealthy, where pernicious malaria was a constant danger... he was always there to restore peace and tranquillity amongst the people who lived in the clutches of terror."

Because of this apostolic Mission the number of brigands began to diminish rapidly. For those who remained, Gaspar appealed to the clemency of the Pope to pardon them if they changed their ways. Pardoning those brigands still at large in the forests would put an end to brigandage. He pointed out that failing to pardon them might bring about acts of desperation; whereas in pardoning them, the Pontiff would also end any new "recruitment" and thus the danger to the local population and to travellers would cease. The money spent on fighting the bandits could be used for works of peace. The Mission Houses would remain behind to minister to the spiritual needs of the people. Gaspar also insisted that all those injustices that had been the root cause of brigandage be brought to an end, particularly the exploitation of the poor.

This initiative of Gaspar's was fought by his adversaries who used diabolic tactics which had the effect of fomenting brigand-age. Unable to oppose the iron will of the Pope, they began to treat those bandits who had turned themselves in with such cruelty, that they caused feelings to run high against Religion and engendered a general refusal to accept the Sacraments before being executed. This is what Gaspar wrote to Castaldi: "I would beseech you to have the Holy Father put an end to the practice of cutting off heads and dismembering bodies... Let

From the confessional Gaspar calls upon a man waiting in line and tells him to hurry to come make his confession. As soon as he returns to his seat, the man dies.

those who have died reconciled to the faith be given a proper burial. In some towns the skulls placed above the doors outnumber the stones!"

When he saw that the promises were not being kept, Gaspar ordered his Missionaries not to become involved in the politics of the Government and not to become intermediaries in any surrenders. They were only to concern themselves with the spiritual needs of the brigands.

His enemies did all they could to make this appear to be an anti–Government stance and Gaspar was even accused of inertia and disobedience. They also had the subsidy granted by Pius VII taken away from the Mission Houses. Since it was a matter which touched not only him personally, but the honour of the Institute, Gaspar defended the work of the Missionaries with all the strength he could muster. They had left everything behind in order to live in the areas most affected by the brigands, risking their lives in the malaria infested marshes, and travelling about the mountains with nothing but a Crucifix in their hands. When the Legate at Frosinone, who headed the opposition against Gaspar summoned him and angrily and arrogantly reproached him, Gaspar answered him calmly and respectfully, but he held his own. The continued existence of brigandage was to be sought not in the alleged fear and ignorance of the Missionaries, but in the hypocrisy, the double dealing and the betrayal of the employees of the state at all levels. Everyone was aware of the fact that the brigands trusted only Gaspar. So much so that one of them, acting as a spokesman for the others, went to Merlini with a letter appealing to Gaspar to act as an intermediary for them with Leo XII in arranging for their surrender and pardon. Gaspar had the letter brought to Castaldi. Leo XII praised the Missionaries and gave the Legate at Frosinone the mandate to negotiate the surrender.

One of Gaspar's missionaries, whose name we already know, wrangled his way into the negotiations in order to claim for himself all the success achieved by Gaspar's apostolate. He went to Gasbarrone dressed as a Missionary and negotiated the surrender. Gasbarrone placed his trust in him. Everyone surrendered but the promises of clemency and a pardon were not kept. Some of them, following Gaspar's advice, left the mountains and lived their lives in hiding as good christians.

On September 9, 1825 Gaspar wrote to Cristaldi that brigandage had come to an end.

THE GREAT REFORMATION

The year 1825 is not only significant in the history of Gaspars's life, but also in the history of the Papal States. This was the year in which the Great Reformation was begun. Gaspar played a significant role in drafting it.

During the period in which Pius VI and Pius VII were in prison, evil men without scruples had outlawed the faith and christian morality. Jacobinism had made its way into the souls of the Romans and had turned them away from religious practices. Nor were matters much better in other parts of the States. "Everything exuded conspiracy and libertinism and, horrible to relate, in those who should have possessed it, the protective barrier of common sense was no longer present." How many wounds there were to heal! How much disorder to be corrected!

Seriously concerned over this state of affairs, Pius VII decided to undertake a radical Reformation and to do it he "called upon Gaspar. He was to be the man of the Reformation". "...since he had given ample proof of the effectiveness of his apostolate, especially in the Marche and in Romagna. The very fact that the Bishops everywhere call upon him to preach Missions and report significant improvements in their dioceses, confirms the correctness of this choice."

Gaspar, in consultation with Cristaldi, sent a preliminary outline entitled, "Reflections on the longed for Reformation", which revealed the depth of his thought, the anguish which filled his heart and his great capabilities as a social reformer. Gaspar's plan, which was later to cause him so much grief, laid bare for the Pontiff the catastrophic moral state of the nation in no uncertain terms and plainly stated the remedies which should be applied without delay.

The Reformation, according to Gaspar, was to begin with the Papal Court, among the Cardinals, Bishops and Prelates, all of whom were not exemplary ministers of the Church. The Clergy had need of holiness and knowledge, the Religious Orders had

O. Scarpelli

to go back to a strict observance of the Rules.

He wanted the bureaucracy to be abolished, its unjust and damaging privileges removed and the delays in meting out justice effectively to the people stopped. He proposed a restructuring of the ecclesiastical and civil offices and putting at their head men who were dignified and qualified to perform the task. He wanted to see the institution of Associations that would give free education to the people and to the young and provide social assistance to the needy. Hospitals and orphanages were to be built. In the Justice system, using only repressive, vindictive and cruel means of dealing with criminals was counterproductive. One must not lose sight of the fact that one was dealing with human beings, worthy of respect, and who, therefore, should be treated charitably. This method would often achieve much better results than ruthlessness. Many of the members of the police force were also in agreement with him and a highly placed officer often said: "What we are unable to get even with a squadron of soldiers, Gaspar is able to achieve with only a sermon!"

Gaspar insisted that the Missionaries of Evil must be fought by the Missionaries of Good who had to dedicate themselves completely to the Missions and "general renewal". For his part, Gaspar consolidated the first two Houses at St. Felix and Pievetorina and then wrote to Cristaldi: "How can we save souls with the Blood of Jesus without the Holy Mission Houses?"

1825 – Never weary or disheartened, Gaspar opened the year with a Mission at Roccagorga. At night he slept little in order to attend to the voluminous mail he received and to the administrative exigencies of the Institute. After Roccagorga he went to Gaeta where, while preaching, he was seen levitating "a few hands above the platform". He held Missions also at Minturno and Castelforte. In the latter they had not thought of providing him lodging and he had to spend the night in the church sleeping

At Castelgandolfo a man wanted at all costs to move through the crowd listening to Gaspar preaching in the piazza. The donkey knelt down and, despite the blows he received from his master, refused to move until the sermon was over.

on a bench. He said: "What greater honour can there be than to be a guest in the House of the Lord?" He did not confine himself to these two towns on this occasion, but went about preaching in the neighbouring areas. He then went to Frosinone to conduct spiritual exercises with a veritable "host" of clerks and thence to Sora for exercises for the clergy followed by a Mission at Ferentino. Although he was seriously ill, he completed this Mission and after the exercises for the Clergy of Arpino , he went to Maenza where the whole series of sermons was centred around devotion to the Most Precious Blood.

If 1825 was a year of joy for the Church because it was a Holy Year, for Gaspar it was a year of tribulation. It was during this period that Gaspar had to fight to keep the name of the Most Precious Blood which he had chosen for the Institute. He defended it as follows in a letter sent to Cristaldi: "This is what our devotion and our name alludes to. This Divine Blood is offered continuously at Holy Mass; it is administered during the Sacraments; it is the price of salvation and, finally, it is the testament of the love of a God made Man." As such it was only fitting. in the mind of this Seraphim and Martyr of the Blood of Jesus, that all mankind should invoke it with recognition and trust, that it not remain a Mystery on which only a few cloistered souls might meditate. The prayers and praises of all of humanity were to be raised to this Divine Blood, because through it, all of mankind has been redeemed. He was so convinced that this Mystery was the foundation of all the others, that he was even ready to shut down all the Houses of the Institute if this name were taken away from it.

But opposition from his enemies grew in a harsh and incred- ible manner. Leo XII, who as a Cardinal had held him in such esteem that he would send his coach to fetch him after his sermons so that he could have him at the palace to converse with him and who, at the beginning of his Pontificate had received him warmly and been supportive of the Congregation, suddenly did a complete about face. Fearing that staying on as head of the Institute was harmful to it, Gaspar contemplated resigning and entrusting the leadership to others. It was St. Vincenzo Pallotti who exhorted him have strength and faith and to carry on as before. The story is told that during this period the Virgin appeared to a pious soul (perhaps Merlini?) and said that: "The Work of Gaspar was under Her maternal protection and She would never allow it to be dismantled." Gaspar would say in turn: "This Work is beloved by God precisely because it is so difficult." Nonetheless, his enemies went too far!

For the first time in his apostolic career, Gaspar was excluded from the group preaching Missions during the Jubilee in Rome. Resigned, he would say: "It doesn't matter for me personally, but this is the Work of God. If they touch my Institute, I shall become a lion!"

The Missionary, Don Innocenzo Betti, at a public audience held in June 1825 presented the Pope with a little book in which he had written a dedication and signed it identifying himself as a Missionary of the Most Precious Blood. The Pope, visibly irritated, crossed out *of the Most Precious Blood* and wrote *of the Most Holy Redeemer*. As soon as Gaspar learned of this episode, he unburdened his exacerbated soul to Cristaldi. The latter was profoundly disturbed by what he heard and decided to intercede and speak freely about it to the Pope. He told Gaspar to return to Rome and not to leave the city under any circumstances because he would do all he could to arrange an audience with the Pope. Gaspar prepared for this encounter with masses, prayers and acts of penitence. He met first with Mons. Soglia, secret Chamberlain of the Pope, to whom he spoke "as though moved by a superior force". It was not he who spoke, but God who spoke through him "and he was moved to tears, because he spoke not for himself, but for the Blood of Christ." And the day of triumph finally arrived. Gaspar had sent the Pontiff three "pro memoria", one on the Institute, one on the Archconfraternity of the Most Precious Blood and the third on the privileges of the Missionaries of the Most Precious Blood.

During the audience, the first words of the Pontiff were harsh and he recapitulated all of the accusations that had been levelled against him. Gaspar became excited and began to speak: he spoke to the Pope like a Seraphim. Leo XII was dumbstruck and completely won over by the Saint's eloquence and asked if he might peruse the Rule briefly. Then he asked Gaspar if he was prepared to accept whatever decision he made on the matter. "I love the Institute more than my own life," Gaspar answered,

"and I'm ready to shed my blood on its behalf. But if Your Holiness orders me to shut down all the Houses I am ready to obey." Upon hearing these words the Pope spread out his arms, embraced Gaspar and said: "You have many enemies, but do not be afraid. Leo XII is on your side." After Gaspar left the room the Pope said: "Canon Del Bufalo is an angel."

Was the ordeal all over then? Gaspar had won, but had his enemies given up? Alas, they had not!

Gaspar took up his proselytizing journey once more and went first to conduct Exercises at Cannara and then to Castelsantangelo and Vizzo. His enemies, having learned how highly Gaspar was regarded by the Pope, now changed their tactics. From a slanderous whisper campaign they began praising his deeds out of all proportion suggesting to the Pope that he elevate him to some high office. They hoped thereby, to remove him from his teaching and his concern for the Institute. Word of these machinations reached Gaspar's ear and from St. Felix he immediately wrote to Cristaldi to plead with the Pope not to take him away from his missionary life. He wanted to die a Missionary and closed his letter with: "I spend days of heavenly bliss among the young pupils in the Boarding School at St. Felix, which is progressing so well. They are a delight to me."

But it was to no avail because in January 1826 he was summoned urgently to Rome. Leo XII received him lovingly and invited him to sit beside him. Gaspar was shaking. What would happen now? The Pope informed him that he had decided to elevate him to the office of Archbishop and to send him as Papal Nunzio to Brazil. Gaspar behaved very circumspectly because he realized it would not be wise to say no right away. He asked for time to pray and to reflect on the matter. He ran immediately to Cristaldi and asked him to implore the Pope not to give him that responsibility. The Pope finally relented but he destined him to the Holy Congregation of the Propaganda Fide so that he might take charge of the serious problem posed by the

At Ariccia, during the procession, a boy who was unable to walk without crutches, breaks away from his mother, clutches the Saint's cassock, and is cured.

Foreign Missions. Gaspar did not dare refuse a second time and bowed his head in obedience. He threw himself into his work with passion since he knew that even there he could do much good and he tried through the Missionaries who went abroad to propagate devotion to the Most Precious Blood throughout the world. As time passed, the pain of not being able to dedicate himself entirely to the work of winning over souls became increasingly hard to bear. As he had predicted, to this sorrow was soon added the loss of Mons. Manasse, Bishop of Terracina and a former missionary. During this period he intensified his missionary and apostolic work around Rome.

His afflictions and his sacrifice were amply rewarded by the Pope who in a public document officially recognized that the name of Gaspar's new Institute would be *The Most Precious Blood of Our Lord Jesus Christ*. The Pope could not have given him a greater gift. The fateful date was July 4, 1826. Things began to change and even the Pope realized that a man with Gaspar's zeal for action could not feel comfortable in the offices of a Ministry, even if it was for the good of so many souls. And so the caged bird regained his freedom to roam about and in December, after a Course of Exercises at Assisi, he went on a Mission to Irpino. Missions, everywhere Missions! He went to Aquila, Sulmona, Castel di Sangro through heavy snow storms and over impossible roads. Thence he travelled to Isernia, among the earthquake victims.

How could he manage to survive, this man, undermined as he was by ill health and so many hardships? He himself tells us: "The ministry makes me as light as a feather. I never feel so well as when I'm on a Mission."

1827 – 1830 – These three years were so filled with hard work and laden down with events that it is difficult to recount everything in a few short paragraphs. In February he hastened to put a stop to the fighting and arguments at Frosinone where the populace feared that the Missionaries would leave. He also

In all the Missions the Saint had people bring immoral prints and fire–arms which would then be burned in the piazza as a sign of the conversions and of peace which had been achieved.

made the necessary preparations for building a House in that city and on March 25 he went back to lay the first stone. He then moved on to Sora for Spiritual Exercises and from there to the Diocesi dei Marsi, which he evangelized in the midst of much-difficulty, penance and fasting. In a letter he mentioned the extreme poverty of the Institute, but he also stated that on a number of occasions "the money had multiplied in his hands" and, moved, he thanked Providence for the miracle. Then followed the Missions at Pietrasecca, Colli, Poggio, Cinolfo, where, while he was preaching in the crowded piazza, a young man who had climbed on an elm tree to see Gasparfell to the ground, Gaspar noticed him from the platform and blessed him. the young man reported no injuries. He went to Albano for some rest... but he preached the entire month on the Most Precious Blood: not only did the faithful come to listen to him in droves, but the Clergy arrived as well, including Cardinal Benedetto Barberini. Despite the stifling heat, he headed for Sermonetta to examine the students there and then he proceeded toward the Diocese of Norcia for Spiritual Exercises for the Clergy and the People. He also went to Pievetorina, where, upon learning that a missionary was dying at Rimini, he hurried to his bedside and said to him: "Come, come. This is no time for staying in bed. There's work to be done." And thus saying he cured him. He also went to preach at Abbazia St. Salvatore near Rieti. After this series of sermons, he continued with another at Pratianni, Coverciano, Vaccareccia and Portigliano; on December 10 he was at Varco and from there he headed toward Roccasinibalda. In most instances we have limited ourselves to mentioning only the names of towns, but we must repeat that where ever he went the crowds flocked to listen to him and on many occasions, in order to move the most obstinate among them, he would scourge himself so that people "were greatly moved".

In January, 1828, he went with Don Biagio Valentini and Don Giovanni Merlini to Poggio Mirteto and then to Castelnuovo, St. Salvatore Maggiore and Fara Sabina, preaching in thirty towns without a break. After so much work, in February he went immediately to Romagna and stayed there for 18 months. From there he wrote to Betti: "The work in Romagna keeps me so busy that I haven't got time to look up. God wants me to stay in

Romagna." He began his proselytizing from Rimini and proceeded on to Cervia, Mondavio, Pennabilli and Soanne. However, he had tried to get out of going to Soanne because he had lost his voice but the parish priest had insisted he should still go. "I will come and say the Rosary if I can't preach." But he regained his voice, as had happened on numerous occasions, and his sermons were "as thunderous as ever". He preached in various other places, among them Macerata Feltria. At Misano, the parish priest was sceptical about his holiness and the marvels that were everywhere being attributed to Gaspar; he therefore kept a close eye on him to see if he could trip him up. One night a bright light could be seen glowing through the cracks in the door of the room where Gaspar was sleeping. The parish priest went to look through the keyhole and saw him rapt in ecstasy before the Crucifix. Also at Misano, Gaspar cured Francesco Pasquini of a malignant tumour. The parish priest saw enough to make him change his mind. At Pennabilli, a mad woman, on seeing him pass by shouted out: "There he is, the stealer of souls!" Here are some other places he went to: St. Agata Feltria, St. Leo and Faenza.

In December, 1828 he congratulated Cristaldi on having been made a Cardinal. In June, 1829 he went to Gaeta again with Merlini on the invitation of Cristaldi and in September he set out for Naples, because the King wanted very much to have in his capital a permanent chapter of the Missionaries of the Most Precious Blood. Gaspar was quite disgusted with the life at court and nothing came of the undertaking.

He ended the year with a series of events, amongst which were Exercises for the Clergy of Benevento which he conducted on the insistence of Cardinal Giovanni Bussi, Archbishop of that city. At the beginning of 1830 he was extremely busy with numerous undertakings in Rome with particular emphasis given to Exercises to a number of Institutes for men and for women. Then he went to Veroli and Ancona. He used this opportunity to make a further visit to the Holy House at Loreto, where he was overwhelmed by the gratitude of the people.

The reader, seeing Gaspar continuously moving about preaching his Missions and thus staying away from Rome for prolonged periods of time, might think that his enemies had finally decided to leave him in peace. On the contrary, if we examine this period closely, we will see that the persecution he was subjected to increased.

While Gaspar was celebrating Mass at the House in Pievetorina, he saw a golden chain descending from the sky into the chalice which had just been consecrated. From there it rose and wound itself around his body. Divine Providence, seeing that so much more suffering had been placed on his shoulders, was consoling him and urging him to accept all that came from its Hand. On Christmas 1827 at Poggio Mirteto, Gaspar was kneeling in ecstasy before the Nativity Scene when he felt himself oppressed by a heavy weight and he had a vision of himself with two enormous crosses on his shoulders. During the vision he saw that he would undergo new and even more terrible trials. This prophecy became a reality almost immediately. In fact the Pope ordered the closing of the Houses at Sonnino and Terracina as a result of the usual slanderous reports.

Gaspar was most distressed that the people of this area who were so in need of the Missions after their experience with the horrors of the brigands, should be thus abandoned to their fate. He wrote: "Let God do with me and with the entire Institute what he will. My only love is that glory be done to Him."

On February 2, 1829 Leo XII died and Gaspar was deeply aggrieved at the loss because this Pope, even if he had caused much grief, had also been of great help to the Institute. He was also upset because "for him and for the Institute a period of suffering was to follow". On March 31 of the same year Pius VIII was elected and under his Papacy Gaspar was to reach the height of his sorrow even if this Pope too, was to have a change of heart.

His enemies, in fact, never let up. The Pope immediately suspended the subsidies to the Houses of Marittima and Campagna. Fortunately, a number of Cardinals who held him in high esteem interceded and soon this decreed was revoked. But there followed hard upon these events a very serious episode. One day while in a group at a public audience with the Pope, Pius VIII recognized him and singled him out and reproached him with harsh words: "Your Institute was born out of arrogance!" And raising his voice he went on: "You, then, are the Founder of the

Institute of the Missionaries of the Most Precious Blood? Have you brought with you the authorization given to you by our predecessor?" Gaspar had not brought the document with him since he could not have foreseen what was happening to him. "You've always acted on your own steam, have you! Well, away with you and be advised that I am removing all authority from you so that you will learn at your own expense to be more humble!" The blow was such that Gaspar had to muster all his strength to keep from fainting. "Recalling all his religious precepts" he regained his composure and went out of the Bronze portals. He had to stop and lean against a column once he was out. In his heart he forgave the Pontiff, whom he knew to be quite ill. Still, there were those about him who could not help gloating and smiling smugly, made fun of him, saying: "There goes the Father General, on his way home empty handed." In his heart, Gaspar kept at bay that feeling of rebelliousness which "the true Enemy" had planted there. Once home, to those about him who noticed how much he was suffering he said only that: "The Pope is ill and did not receive me warmly." And as he often did, he hurried to relate his woes to Cardinal Cristaldi. With his help and that of a number of other Cardinals who took his side, and after a humble letter sent to Pius VIII, the latter had a change of heart and said: "We shall see about making a place for this Institute. I bless it daily every time I raise up the Chalice at Holy Mass." However, he did not have enough time to put his good intentions into practice because he died on November 30, 1830, just 20 months after having acceded to the Papacy. When he learned of his death, Gaspar was much aggrieved and he said to those present: "The successor of Pius VIII will reign long and well. After him, under another Pontiff, the Church will go through many tribulations and there will be much bloodshed." Unfortunately, his prophesy was to prove to be quite accurate.

A dispute arose over the dress of the brothers and even some of the more educated and renowned among them disagreed with him on this issue. However, among holy men, righteous and intelligent people, the truth will always win out. And thus, without ill feelings, harmony was restored. After a great deal of thought on all sides and letters from Gaspar everyone agreed that he was right after all.

1831 – During this year Cardinal Mauro Cappellari was elected Pope. He was a man with a strong and loyal personality and took the name of Gregory XVI. Gaspar appealed to his friend, Cardinal Carlo Odescalchi, to speak to the new Pontiff about his Institute. On April 20 the Cardinal informed him that the Pope "had been forewarned and was opposed to the very foundation of the Institute itself". He therefore, not only was not interested in hearing about the Rule, but he was set on eliminating all subsidies to the Houses. Rey says of this news: "A knife through the heart would have been less painful. Nonetheless, as usual, Gaspar turned to the Crucifix. Not even the slander which had reached the ear of this Pope would be enough to undo the Work which God had willed. Providence would, in due course, see to it that the Rule was approved."

The world was undergoing turbulent times. In France the Bourbons had been deposed. Poland was stirring and rumours filled the air of plots against the Papal Government aimed at destroying it. There were insurrections in Emilia and Romagna and the populace of Marche and Umbria were in a constant state of agitation.

Gaspar remained serene amidst all this rattling of sabres and continued on placidly with his work as an apostle, concerned only with the spiritual health of the souls he ministered to. It was unfortunate that at the beginning of his reign, even this Pope was against him. And yet he would be remembered as the Pope of the Missions.

During this year Gaspar was to suffer the loss of two of the people dearest to him. His beloved father died, as did his great friend and protector, Cardinal Bellisario Cristaldi. He attended to the burial of his father with loving care. In the courtyard of our House at Piazza dei Crociferi in Rome the memorial tablet is still preserved with the epitaph he composed and which was to have been placed on his tomb in the church of St. Adriano a Campo Vaccino in Rome. It is difficult to say whether he suffered more over the loss of his father or that of Cristaldi. With the latter he lost the father of his Institute, a true friend and a reliable helping hand in dark and difficult moments. He had solemn and pious services celebrated on his behalf and recorded in the archives that he was among the Institute's greatest benefactors, thus ensuring his memory would be revered in perpetuity by those who came after him.

These sorrows were mitigated by some happy occurrences which the Lord granted him. He opened the House at Nepi near Viterbo in November 1831 and the one at Macerata Feltria in Romagna on May 28, 1831. He also had the joy of seeing the House at Sonnino reopened (Dec. 1832). In 1831 he held a second Mission at Sezze along with Valentini, Aloisi and Fontana. They were welcomed by all the children of the little town with the cry of "Long Live Mary". He also held a course of Exercises in the Monastero di Gesùe Maria in Albano, where in 1838, a year after his death, he was to perform a significant miracle. We leave out numerous other localities.

1832 – In February he was at Orte and in June at Civitella Castellana, where he preached to Nuns, the clergy, military personnel and various other groups. In August he went to Sermonetta where the inhabitants from Norma and Bassiano came to listen to him. It was at Sermonetta, while he was in the confessional, that he pointed to a man who seemed confused among the crowd of those waiting their turn to confess, and said: "Let him come up now, for he needs to confess right away." After confessing the man died in the church in the presence of all those who had witnessed the event.

1833 – If for 1831 and 1832 we have not given the names of many places, it is not because Gaspar went only to those places mentioned. We have left out many localities for the sake of brevity or because it was felt that it would be superfluous to mention them since we have included many of them earlier on. But Gaspar was continually pressed by requests from parish priests and bishops, even from those towns where he had already held a Mission because they remembered the good that had come of them.

At the beginning of 1833 he went to Palestrina and Zagarolo where his conversion of a woman who had refused to forgive the young man who had killed her daughter became legendary. The young man was in prison and had repented, asking for her forgiveness. After the persuasive words of the Saint and his emotional sermon, the woman threw herself weeping into his arms and offered her forgiveness. At Palestrina he cured a servant of Prince Rospigliosi of epilepsy. Thence he went to Genazzano, but he was unable to complete the Mission because of a serious illness. After a few days of rest, he went in April to Veroli. The press spoke at length of this Mission because of the large number of conversions, the feuds resolved and the destruction of obscene prints and fire–arms. During this year he also preached at Guarcino, Palestrina, Poggio Mirteto, Converciano and Ronciglione.

His health continued to deteriorate and in 1834 he remained at length at Albano where, however, he taught Theology to the pupils and preached spiritual exercises to the people and the Religious Communities in the area. He visited, as prescribed by the Rule, the various Houses of the Institute and in August he was in Forlimpopoli. Although this was one of the more turbulent towns of Romagna, Gaspar had a particular affection for it and gladly dedicated a large part of his apostolate to it. He was amply rewarded by the enthusiasm and the affection which the populace lavished on him and he performed quite a few marvels here. From Forlimpopoli, as usual, he went to the nearby Meldola which insisted that he visit.

In 1835 he took part in ministries in Rome, Port of Anzio, Cori and Velletri. During the summer he revised the Rules of the Institute for the last time. He would have liked to submit them to the Pope for his approval but he was counselled against it because the Pope did not yet approve of the Institute.

In 1836 he preached a Mission at Todi which was to remain among the more memorable ones. He also went to preach spiritual exercises to the people of Cori, where he cured a possessed nun and a little girl whose feet were paralysed. From Cori he went on a Mission to Priverno and at the end of the year to Nepi where he contracted the whooping cough which stayed with him till his death. At the beginning of 1837 he went to Port of Anzio again to preach spiritual exercises to the populace and to the inmates of the prison there.

After preaching at Anzio, Gaspar and his companions set out on the return journey to Bassiano. Brother Bartolomeo, although not very familiar with the area, suggested they take a short cut. Unfortunately, the road turned out to be boggy and unsuitable for a carriage to travel on. Suddenly the vehicle leaned to one side and slid more than half way into the swampy ground. To make matters worse it was raining very heavily. The horses bolted and broke free of their harness. Some of the Missionaries were almost suffocated and Gaspar suffered a severe contusion to the head. When they pulled him out he was in convulsions and barely able to stand up. He was accompanied on foot and without an umbrella through the heavy rain to the House at Sermonetta where he was put to bed with a high fever. And then, for those unfamiliar with Gaspar's zeal and strength of will, something unbelievable happened. In his state of health, he got up the following morning and took part in the Mission at Bassiano during which he shouldered all the attending difficulties "heroically concealing and scorning his infirmity ".

By now his life was seriously threatened. From that time on he remained afflicted by a dry, convulsive cough. After Easter he retired to Albano and put the finishing touches on the Rule. He was often found sitting at his desk, his gaze fixed on an small painting of the Sorrowful Mother, tears streaming down his cheeks.

To his brothers he would say: "Soon I will no longer be a burden to you. I am preparing for myself for eternity."

THE DEATH OF GASPAR
THE APOTHEOSIS
THE SAINT

O. Scarpelli

THE DEATH OF GASPAR

1837 – This was the year, as Gaspar had predicted years earlier, in which the plague struck the city of Rome. While everyone was fleeing the Eternal City to take refuge in the Castelli Romani, Gaspar, an angel of charity, inspired by love for his fellow citizens who were in the clutches of so horrible a scourge, left Albano and rushed into the city. He could barely stand, yet he contintued to help the plague's victims with all the energy he could muster. He went from house to house bringing the last spiritual comforts to the sick, as well as food and medicine to those who were still alive. Heedless of the danger of contamination, he was also seen carrying on his shoulders, corpses which had been abandoned in the street and loading them onto the carts which would then take them to be buried. The Pope ordered sanitary measures to be undertaken and took part in a procession of penitence dressed in sack cloth. The Madonna del Popolo was carried, accompanied by an enormous crowd of the faithful, from St. Maria Maggiore to St. Peter in the Vatican. In the major churches in Rome propitiatory rites were performed and the most renowned preachers were instructed ascend to the pulpits and ask the faithful to repent. The Cardinal Vicar of Rome, unaware of Gaspar's precarious state of health,

The Death of Gaspar

assigned him to the Chiesa Nuova, where the remains of St. Filippo Neri were venerated. It was the month of August and stifling hot. Gaspar dragged himself along and it was painful to see him struggling up the steps of the pulpit. Yet, once he began preaching in front of so many people, in the presence of the authorities, prelates and cardinals, he seemed to be charged with the apostolic fervour of old. He moved everyone to tears. As soon as he had finished his sermon, he was overcome by a bout of coughing which would not go away and as soon as he got to his room he threw himself exhausted onto his tiny bed. The Filippini Fathers with whom he was staying and who were affectionately taking care of him, advised him to take a break from his preaching. He answered: "I have always prayed the Lord to let me die while preaching from the pulpit." Between one bout of coughing and the next he recited short prayers.

Once his preaching assignment was over, the doctor ordered him to go back to the milder climate at Albano. Gaspar obeyed, even though he knew that his time had come whether he went to Rome or stayed at Albano. Had he not foreseen his end many times over down to the smallest detail.

On November 18, he signed his papers for the last time and handed them over to the Venerable Merlini with the words: "Let everything remain unchanged." He spent most of his time in an easy chair or lying on the bed in his room. When weather permitted, he would be accompanied, supported on either side, for a walk in the garden.

He gathered up all the energy in his spirit during this period so that he could remain in constant union with God. He would raise his eyes towards the sky and repeat over and over: "Heaven! Heaven! Shall I be among the saved?" Those who were with him would ask: "If you won't be saved, who can aspire to salvation?" And he would answer: "I am but a poor sinner!" His spiritual testament during these last days was, as he constantly repeated to everyone, is summarized in three phrases: Love for God; Jesus and Mary; his Congregation. Here is his solemn oath, modelled on a biblical expression: "May my right hand wither away if I should be forgetful of you, O Congregation of the Most Precious Blood!"

With the first signs of cold weather, his state of health became visibly worse. Cardinal Franzoni, protector of the Institute and a great friend and admirer of Gaspar's learned of his condition and ordered him to return to Rome. Thus he went to live in the very modest apartment which he had rented in the building built onto the ancient Theatre of Marcellus and there he remained till the end of his life. He took to his bed only when he was too weak even to remain in the easy chair. Since he could no longer celebrate Mass now, he had Holy Communion brought to him every day. His faithful servant, Bartolomeo, never moved from his bedside. Gaspar was greatly moved when he received a Nativity Scene which the Sisters of St. Urbano had made for him out of paper. He had it placed on the large chest in front of his bed and exclaimed: "My God, my God, how much love for us!"

His condition deteriorated even further and because of his high fever, the doctor recommended that he be bled. Gaspar had prophesied that when they bled him he would die, yet he agreed to the procedure. His enemies gave him no rest even on his death bed. They let it be known that he was afraid of dying and that he was despairing. His childhood friend, Sister Maria Tamini, on hearing this, rushed to his bedside to comfort him. Gaspar reassured both her and Merlini, who was at his side and who had asked him if he were "at peace with the Divine will". He received Extreme Unction and murmured: "Now I am content." He entered into agony.

In addition to Bartolomeo, his niece Gigia was with him. Vincenzo Pallotti was present and he has left this testimony: "The sick man seemed to be in a state of perfect serenity and on his face there shone such sweetness, joy and such signs of peace, that, from a christian point of view, one was tempted to want to be experiencing the agony." And he adds: "As though imbued with heavenly joy, he expired calmly and quietly." It was two o'clock in the afternoon of December 28, 1837.

Pallotti himself revealed later that he had seen the soul of Gaspar in the guise of a shining star rising up to heaven as Jesus and the Virgin came down to meet him. In fact, those present had seen Pallotti staring fixedly upward and exclaiming: "Blessed soul, already you are in Heaven."

How many times during his life had Gaspar raised his eyes towards heaven and exclaimed: "Heaven!" How many times had he desired it ardently as he gazed at the starry sky! How many times in his suffering and in refusing honours and praise had he said: "Heaven! Heaven!"

Finally he was climbing, flying upwards to take his place in the Heaven he had so fervently desired and so richly deserved.

THE APOTHEOSIS

To his elevation to Heaven was added that of his being raised in stature here on earth. His ascent towards sainthood began at Albano, where his body was transferred on the evening of December 31, after solemn ceremonies at Rome at St. Angelo in Pescheria.

His followers were so eager to see the face of their beloved Gaspar, that the coffin was opened right away and everyone observed with awe and joy that, despite the fact that four days had passed from his death, his body was still supple and flexible and gave off a mysterious fragrance. On New Year's Day he reposed in the church in an open coffin. As the news spread the crush of people was unbelievable. Everyone wanted to see him, touch him, have something of his to keep. One individual even tried cutting off one of his fingers. In the first three days of January, solemn funeral masses were held. The church was filled to bursting and the square crowded with the faithful. Many people who were ill had been brought there hoping to obtain a miracle. They were not to be disappointed.

We list briefly some of the fortunate ones.

A nun from Cori saw him, at the moment of his death, getting up and flying towards heaven. Another nun saw St. Francis Xavier going to meet him immediately after his death. A priest at Sezze, while celebrating mass, saw him flying towards heaven. There is also a story about a highly placed person of the time having had a similar vision.

Raimondo Marazzi was cured of pernicious fevers; the little grandson of Clementina Bugiaferri, crippled and mute, ran all around the church shouting for joy; Orsola Pietrangeli had her cheek healed; Orsola Mazzani was relieved of the terrible pains in her head; a young man prostrated himself before the body and his syphilis disappeared; the stone mason who had been commissioned to prepare the crypt in the church was cured of rheumatic pains which had been unbearable.

Since after seven days of being on exhibit in the church the body of Gaspar remained flexible and rosy and emitted a sweet fragrance, some people began suspecting that it had been embalmed. The body was thus thoroughly examined by a Medical Committee and its findings were unequivocal: there had been no such treatment and the phenomenon was, therefore, completely natural. The corpse was then placed in a wooden coffin, sealed and buried in the church, beneath the altar where the saint is now venerated. Two years later the body was exhumed and discovered to be still intact. It was then placed in two coffins, a wooden one within a lead one, and buried again in the same place.

His fame as a Saint did not die with him, but increased greatly. From Cardinals, Princes and Bishops, down to the most humble, people began to flock to his sepulchre from all parts of Italy to ask for his intercession. Gaspar responded with much generosity to the requests of those that were devoted to him.

We shall relate a few incidents which have been objectively verified. Pallotti says that Princess Massima Ruspoli who had remained childless, was able to experience the joy of motherhood by carrying about with her a relic of the Saint. Merlini relates that Count Soderini of Rome was cured of a serious condition, a ruptured hernia, by placing the relic of the Saint on the affected area of his body. Merlini also relates that a certain Francesca Tolomeo had turned cold and was on the verge of giving up the ghost; by invoking the name of Gaspar she recovered immediately and was cured. At Rimini the parish priest of St. Nicola in Porto told the story that his parishioner, Mariano Ballerini, affected by a serious case of dropsy, was cured by invoking St. Gaspar. Don Giovanni Palmucci wrote from Ascoli Piceno to Merlini that Sister Costanza Villati was cured of horrible convulsions, after having invoked the Servant of God, Gaspar Del Bufalo. Again, Merlini relates that a son of Agnese Marazza of Castelgandolfo was cured of a cyst which had swollen over his right eye to the size of a large nut. The wonder occurred while the woman was praying in the church where the Saint was buried. Dr. Marcutelli of Sezze Romano

O. Scarpelli

relates that Sister Eletta Margherita De Cesaris was cured of a mortal disease of the stomach after swallowing a Relic of the Servant of God. Don Girolamo Sciamplicotti of the parish of Rocca di Papa tells the moving story of how his parishioner, M. Antonia D'Ottavio was cured of excruciating pain to her teeth after going to pray at the tomb of St. Gaspar. Cecilia Marlotti of Castelgandolfo, seriously ill, was cured after she had prayed and asked for the intercession of St. Gaspar. The following were also cured by invoking the name of St. Gaspar: Giacomo Vicino of Castelgandolfo, who had a malady in his neck; Stefano Mondelli of Rome, in the final stages of tuberculosis; Gaetano Biagioli, suffering from severe haemoptysis (spitting up blood from lungs); Sister Costanza Rolli of Monte Carignano, who was near death; Maria Falcetti of Rome, who had a tumour of the brain.

Merlini also narrates that Agostino Bianchi, during the cholera epidemic at Albano, was already dead and they gathered him up to take him to be buried. His three year old daughter grabbed onto her father's body and yelled out: "Give him the image of St. Gaspar to eat!" After the image was placed in his mouth, the "dead man" opened his eyes and said: "I went to the gates of eternity but they refused to let me in." Sister Maria Maddalena della Trinita gave testimony concerning the cure of her vicar, Sister M. Giuseppina, from a tumour to the stomach, bronchial asthma and pneumonia. Don Carlo Lattanzi, parish priest at Civitalavinia, testified to the cure of Pietro Paolo Pochino from a serious bout of pernicious malaria after taking a relic of the Saint. The miracle performed on Maria De Maistre has remained famous. She was a Sister of the Daughters of Mercy of St. Vincent De Paul and was so crippled that the sole of one of her feet lay against her hip and required that the leg be amputated. She was cured after invoking the name of the Venerable man and swallowing his relic. Another miracle took place in Paris. The nobleman Giorgio Schouvanoff of Petersburg had a daughter who was so paralyzed that she had to

The cure of Ottaviano Lo Stocco, the first miracle for the beatification.

spend her life in a wheelchair. After hearing of the miracle received by De Maistre, he asked for a relic of the Venerable man and, after a novena to the Most Precious Blood, he had the sick girl swallow it. She was cured on the spot.

We bring to an end here the brief list, regretting that we have to omit so many others. Later on we will look at the miracles approved for his beatification and his canonization.

These events, duly confirmed by and large by doctors and other trustworthy persons, along with the persistent requests on the part of Bishops, Prelates, Cardinals and the people themselves, moved the Church to establish in the various parishes where the Saint had been and at Rome an *Inquiry into the reputation for saintliness, the heroic virtues practised by the Saint and the miracles performed by him.*

Let us also look more closely, along with the Church, at the unparalleled virtue of Gaspar so that we may admire him, imitate him and invoke his name.

THE SAINT

In order to be a Saint there are two prerequisites: Divine Grace, without which any worthy action is impossible, and the positive will of the person. Grace is never absent for those who have been baptised, but human beings are not always up to the task. There is no doubt that Gaspar was enriched by many gifts conferred upon him by Grace and munificently lavished on him by a sanctifying God. And this Grace greatly facilitated his journey along the path of virtue. But it is equally true that Gaspar on his part responded to the call and made of himself a humble instrument in its hands. As we have seen, he was not spared numerous harsh trials which he overcame by by the heroism of his virtues, which shone through in his every action and in all circumstances.

Of the virtues, the supernatural gifts, and the Miracles of the Saint, we have already spoken in various parts of his biography so far. The reader will likely find some repetition in what follows. But we too, like the great historians such as Sardi, Rey and others, wish to give a brief synthesis of his life at this point so that the reader will have a clearer picture of the stature of this great man and Saint.

St. Vincenzo M. Strambi defined St. Gaspar as "A man full of Faith and the Holy Spirit". Born and raised in Rome where, it may be said, every stone and every clump of earth has been watered by the tears of many Saints and stained by the blood of the Martyrs, he too felt impelled to consecrate his life to the Lord and yearned to give his life for the Faith and spend it among the faithful. He asked two things of the Lord: "To be able to die preaching and to give his blood for the Faith." He was threatened many times during his ministry, yet he continued on unswervingly, saying: "To die for Christ is a Victory!" This was not only because his sight had been miraculously cured by the intercession of St. Francis Xavier. He had also been enraptured by the life of this great missionary, became devoted to him and chose him as the Patron Saint of his Congregation. "There was also too much of India [i.e. poverty, non–believers, etc.] in Rome and in Italy." It was for this reason that he founded the Congregation of the Missionaries of the Most Precious Blood. He wanted many men of God to dedicate their entire lives to bringing faith and love to the people and to bringing back to God so many souls that had moved away from him.

He was an Apostle for his times, sent by God. As in their day, St. Francis, St. Domenic, St. Ignatius and others had been sent. And he threw himself headlong into the work of the Missions which he held to be the most fitting way of converting sinners.

Jacobinism, Freemasonry and other sects were becoming widespread and infecting the world. His apostolic action was so tireless, courageous and fertile that he became known as the *Hammer of the Heretics*. He preferred to take his message to the masses and he was partial to the poor and the humble, to whom he taught, even as a boy, the truth about the Faith and what they had to do in order to be saved. His doctrine was closely linked to that of the Church. His knowledge of sacred matters was so great and his ability in apologetics and dialectic was so refined that he could refute any erroneous argument against the Faith and morals with only a few words. One remained awestruck at a man who was so timid by nature, resisting with such vehemence the attempts at intimidation by judges. "He would take up his position like a giant and when he went to do battle with his adversaries, he seemed to be totally absorbed and his face was ablaze, because he was constantly in the presence of God." Others said of him: "He seemed like an angel." His thirst for souls was such that he "undertook perilous journeys, braving all kinds of inclement weather and not infrequently in our intractable mountains". He was wont to say that he would have given up his own life to save a soul. And he gave proof of it through his actions. There was no obstacle which could stand in the way of his zeal.

His words, simple as they were, strengthened by his faith and the ardour of his spirit, were penetrating, illuminating, convincing: "God has deigned to impart to me, miserable sinner that I am, a special insight into matters pertaining to apologetics and the truth of our Faith." It is therefore, not surprising that he obtained so many conversions. "The number of converts were legion!" He instilled in his companions the same kind of fervour, stressing the privilege which had been conferred on them by God in having been called upon to bring the faith to the people and he urged them to suffer out of love for Christ.

This fervent activity was the outward manifestation of his inner life. "God sees me," he repeated often. "We do everything for His Glory" and therefore "he was continuously absorbed with God." He could not bear blasphemy, he had pornographic and blasphemous prints destroyed and distributed holy images and books in their place. He did all he could to eradicate gambling houses.

Since Christ, especially for a priest, is made flesh during the celebration of Mass and present in the Tabernacle, his devotion to the Eucharist was great. When he stood before the Most Holy Sacrament, such was his concentration..."that he seemed like a Seraphim". "When he entered a church, he seemed to become someone else, such were the faith and the piety with which he became imbued." "Thus he insisted on the greatest respect and concentration in church and that they be kept spotless. He wanted the altar to be always decorated with fresh flowers and the sacred ornaments should always display a certain decorum." "I would like to see them kept like a jewel!" He would sweep and dust himself and teach his Pupils that they must take the utmost care of their temple and the sacred objects. He also required a strict observance of all the liturgical rules. For him, the Most Holy Sacrament was at the centre of his spiritual life.

He was happy and proud to be a priest and made long preparations for celebrating Holy Mass and his gratitude at being able to do so was great. He always celebrated the anniversary of his ordination to the priesthood with great joy and he had the greatest respect and consideration for all priests, even the least worthy. He would visit the Most Holy every day and when he could "he would spend hours absorbed" in prayer before the Tabernacle. He was very concerned at the progress of his pupils because they were one day to become worthy priests. He worked very hard to find candidates with a suitable vocation.

Wherever he went to preach, he would set up, if it did not already exist, the Confraternity of the Most Holy Sacrament and the pious practice of Perpetual Adoration. He never missed an opportunity for celebrating Holy Mass. He did it "with great devotion", "his face ablaze", his cheeks lined with tears, "in deep concentration for many hours after the Consecration". The faithful that attended his masses would say: "Let us go listen to a mass said by a Saint."

"The most sacred and most spotless vessel," he was wont to say, "must be our soul." "Thus he would go to confession often, even if, as everyone asserted, he had never fallen into the error of sin and had kept intact the innocence with which he had received the sacrament of baptism."

He was extremely attached to the Church and its laws and as we know, it was because of this loyalty that he suffered exile and imprisonment. He never disobeyed Ecclesiastical Authority, because, even if at times the orders seemed to be or actually were unjust, he held them to be a emanation of the Divine Will. In order not to oppose the instructions of various Popes, he suffered through many hardships and painful injustices.

"His heart," says Bragaglia, "was a furnace of love, beating solely for God and for his neighbour." There are thousands of such affirmations which have survived. "His soul belonged truly to God," Merlini states. "He loved God intensely," De Mattias said. One had to listen to him when he spoke of God. One was enchanted and remained echanted in hearing and seeing him pray. He would often be in ecstasy, as we shall see.

This great love drove him to speak always of God. How willingly we speak of the things we love! "Send me Your grace and Your love, my God and I will seek no further." Here is one of his maxims: "He who loves God speaks little, works much, takes everything and gives everything." And St. Vincenzo Strambi suggests: "It is God who is speaking through the mouth of Canon Del Bufalo."

It is quite natural that since such a flame burned within him, he would set others ablaze. While he was still a young student, he would go to various parts of Rome to teach catechism to children and to the people in general. As time went on, and after he had become a priest, this activity became the principal scope of his existence. All that we have said so far of his Missions is little more than the expression of his zeal for the glory of God and his concern for the salvation of souls. It was not enough to simply speak to the masses in general; he had specific sermons of instruction for the various classes in society. He went everywhere, even on the boats of fishermen, into gambling houses, to meeting places, hospitals and prisons. For everyone he had the right thing to say and an appropriate example. Famous and learned men listened to him willingly. His sermons in Rome were attended by Bishops and Cardinals. Leo XII, on his way through Barberini Square where Gaspar was addressing a crowd, stopped his coach so he could listen to him. People from all walks of life and highly placed persons flocked to him to hear his words of advice. Many sinners became converted, many just persons became more perfect and many priests turned from a life of inaction to one of active and apostolic activity. A number of them became his followers.

He didn't stop at giving advice and offering words of consolation. He used to say that: "We are all like patients in a large hospital" and in his father's tender heart all of the sufferings of humanity found a place: from divine love, to love of his neighbour, for whose benefit he dedicated his entire life. In the medical certificate drawn up on the cause of his premature death we read: "Because he would not stop his apostolic activity, he neglected taking the precautionary actions at the beginning which could have been beneficial to him: he thus became a victim of his own love."

In imitation of Christ, he practised the greatest of mercy towards sinners, even if he severely condemned the sin. He would say to those hearing confessions: "How merciful God is! See to it that you too, are merciful!" He considered himself worthy of every conceivable scorn. And indeed, he was a martyr of persecutions, of slander, of calumny; and yet, he forgave everyone. He did all he could to bring peace between enemies, family members, and whole towns. He went to prisons and hospitals, sat next to the most disgusting patients, he helped comfort those who were dying, and said prayers for their souls. "He sees about him the naked that must be clothed, the poor who hold out their hands for a piece of bread, people who knock at his door and at the doors of his Mission Houses and he does all he can to alleviate their misery. He goes from house to house begging for the poor under his care." He used to say: "To do good you must have God's grace as well as money." How often he would sneak into the house so that his brothers would not see that he had given away to the poor even his shoes and the clothes off his own back! One night he was discovered carrying his straw mattress to the house of a sick man. He would visit wretched hovels bringing with him some benediction, a word of comfort and faith, or some small offering of charity, depending on the circumstances. His Rule made it mandatory that no poor person who came knocking at the door of the Mission House must ever be sent away without a plate of hot soup and a bit of money. Once he severely reprimanded the brother at the door who had treated a beggar badly, saying: "Is this how you treat Jesus Christ?" Even in the places where he went to preach, he founded the Ristretti delle Sorelle della carit! which were to dedicate themselves to assisting the sick, the poor and those who were in prison. We quote here a particularly significant passage: "He was suffering in the extreme, and with his own litany of physical maladies that tormented him constantly, with a swollen vein in his foot, afflicted with asthma and continuous pain from his teeth, he could well appreciate the seriousness of the ills which pressed down on humanity. Yet he was always more concerned with the sufferings of others than his own, and he always considered them to be worse off than himself." This was truly a heroic way of practising love for one's neighbour.

THE ATTRACTION OF HIS VIRTUES

St. Gaspar may be referred to by the phrase which the Gospel uses for St. Joseph: a just man. The world easily forgets the values of the spirit, tramples on them and mocks them. That is why the Lord sends to the Church such outstanding personages whose virtues we find so attractive.

Gaspar was a perfect example of justice: each person must be treated as an individual according to his needs and capabilities. "He was just towards God, fulfilling to the utmost all his duties, and just towards his neighbour." He sought to be perfect in his actions and he was the first to adhere strictly to the Rule of the Congregation which he himself had dictated and he repeated to everyone: "It is God's will that we become saints!" He was very precise in meting out just retribution where it was due; he was never niggardly in paying what was asked if the price was fair; he was ever grateful towards his Benefactors and prayed for them and had prayers said on their behalf.

He was strong in shouldering whatever trials were sent his way, but he was equally robust in defending the rights of his Institute and those of the poor and the weak. We have seen with what courage he opposed those who, in his fight against the brigands, resorted to methods which ran contrary to christian charity and justice. For himself, he accepted with humility and courage all adversities that came his way without uttering a word of reproach against those who would persecute him. He never defended himself except when it was necessary to do so to save the honour of the Congregation and his fellow brothers. He bore the humiliating episodes with heroism, and there were many of them, even from his own followers in the Institute; he, too, as we have indicated, had his own Judas to contend with.

How often he was offended and persecuted by those very people who should have defended him and who had been helped by him. In Romagna his patience was so renowned that the following saying is still popular: "I don't quite have the patience of Canon Del Bufalo." To those who complained when things did not go their way, he used to say: "Let's let God take care of it." Here is someone's testimony: "There was in him great fortitude of spirit, whether it was in travelling, preaching, confessing, putting up with adversity, running the Institute, the

Missions, convincing the unbelievers, overcoming temptation, eradicating abuse and scandal." He made his own the words pronounced to the apostles. "Let us go with joy, for we have been made worthy of suffering for Christ." "If the Cross were lacking, Christ's inheritance would be lacking."

He was obedient to the extreme and he would say: "Obedience is the royal road to heaven!" He did not include in his Rule the vows of obedience and poverty, however, he stated: "Let others take vows, we will observe them."

Do you recall that he told Pope Leo XII that he was ready to shut down all the Houses of the Institute if he had ordered him to do so? It would doubtless have caused him immense sorrow, but he was prepared to obey.

He loved poverty; if he needed, collected or accepted money, it was only to use it for the poor. "He refused positions that would have brought rich rewards, generous donations for masses, bequests and lavish gifts. "He died in extreme poverty, insisting that all his riches were contained in the Crucifix." And he also insisted that his Congregation remain poor and he would have been saddened if it had been born in wealth. If it were to become rich, he would have disowned it. Still he did all in his power to ensure that nothing of necessity was ever lacking. And the Congregation was indeed poor, so much so that at times there was not even enough bread and out of necessity the brothers had not infrequently to go out into the rain with only one umbrella for three of them! He would exhort them: Have faith, Providence will not fail us." On not a few occasion, he resorted to performing miracles; in fact we have already related that he used to say that, he did not know how, but God was always ready to pay his debts.

His soul's most beautiful ornament was his purity, which he maintained intact, just as he had received it at the baptismal font. They called him "The celestial Del Bufalo." He was very strong in resisting that "mass of temptations" with which the devil assailed him; nor were there lacking individuals who tried to tempt him into sinning. Once a woman was sent to tempt him, but he quickly discovered the deceit. Still, he must have felt rather unsure of himself because he would have been lost had it not been for a crown of chalices which always surrounded him

O. Scarpelli

and protected him from the devil who wanted to devour him. He used every precaution: he was modest, polite, reserved, he mortified himself with fasts, hair shirts, self–flagellation and above all, he prayed. The Lord appreciated and rewarded this purity. From his chastity there emanated such a fragrance that many of the penitent came away from his confessional exclaiming: "Oh! What a fragrance emanates from that Servant of God. Don Domenico Giorgi of Bassiano asserted that even the room he lived in "exuded an odour of paradise".

HIS GIFTS

God, almost always, whether to reward their virtues or that unbelievers may believe and the faithful be strengthened in their faith and exalt the power of the Lord, often gives his Saints supernatural gifts and the power to perform miracles. Had not Jesus said to the unbelievers, as he performed his miracles: "If you do not want to believe in me, believe in my works"? And had he not also said: "He who believeth in me, he too shall perform the works that I perform and greater ones still." "Gaspar was not lacking such gifts, indeed he possessed them in abundance even if, being so humble, he tried to keep them hidden. These gifts were a new reward with which God wished to repay him for all the immense hardship he underwent.

He had the gift of preaching "with which he stole hearts". "His Missions were accompanied by celestial blessings." "Wherever he preached, people flocked to hear him full of enthusiasm" even from far away towns, neglecting their own interests and occupations. The results, as we have had many occasions to relate, were extraordinary, stupendous. Mounds of confessions, enormous sums of stolen money returned, age–old disputes resolved, reconciliations between individuals and whole towns where people had been divided by inveterate hatred, families that were dispersed were reunited, blasphemy was uprooted, everywhere good manners blossomed, entire areas

Clementina Masini is cured, the second miracle accredited for his beatification

were transformed, deadly weapons and obscene prints were burned and destroyed in the presence of the image of the Our Lady of the Most Precious Blood, heretics who recanted, individuals who abandoned their scandalous behaviour and took refuge in cloisters to atone for their sins. To obtain such amazing results he used no stratagems, no theatricals; the ardour of his words, at times accompanied by self–flagellation, was sufficient to move his listeners. Everyone present felt he was talking to them personally. Many confessed that they were unable hold back their feelings of remorse after having listened to him. Some said that when he pointed to the wounds of the Crucifix, they felt the pain in their own souls. It was not a momentary occurrence. The goodness he promoted and the conversions he obtained were lasting. On many occasions the hardships, the bad weather and the stress drained him of strength and he lost his voice. Yet, as he was about to preach, his energy returned and his voice carried far and wide. Miraculously, it was also heard at great distances. As we have already recounted, at Forlimpopoli a number of Sectarians had gone away to have a good time in a nearby villa and had barred the windows. Still, they heard him as though he were just outside. They came back to the square to hear him preaching and were subsequently converted. At Comacchio, there were visitors from other countries present when he preached. Yet each understood him in his own tongue. At Mergo, a star hovered over his head while he spoke in the square and disappeared after his sermon. At Belforte, as at Pentecost, tongues of fire descended on him and on the people. As he preached, he would calm storms, stop the rain or the snow. These things happened in various places; Albano Laziale, Chiaravalle, Castelfidardo, St. Salvatore, Ascoli Piceno, Cori, Caldarola and Spello, to mention only a few. At Rieti, while he was preaching to the people, and in the presence of the Bishop, a mysterious, shining dove flew about his head and then, while he spoke in the Duomo, a flash of lightning out of a clear sky darted across the vault of the church without harming anyone or causing any damage.

Gaspar also had the gift of *reading consciences*, as well as the hearts and minds of many people, thereby uncovering their intimate secrets. Many people have testified to the truth of this fact. A certain Teresa Spezzaferro declared that, having come to the confessional, Gaspar told her everything that her heart contained and the intimate secrets of her life, before she had said a word. He "revealed his intimate thoughts" to Don Vittoria Tagliaferri. Santelli writes: "He laid bare whatever one was thinking." He read the most secret thoughts of many of his own Missionaries. At Cannara, while talking to the Missionaries, he pointed to one of them and told him that he would leave the Institute. He confessed that to be precisely what he was thinking about at that very moment. Even Merlini states that Gaspar read his most intimate thoughts and that he had proof of it. To the Sisters of Jesus and Mary at Albano he said: "How many devils there are both within and without the walls of this monastery." It was true. He informed Don Antonio Mancini of his mother's death when it happened even though she was far from where they were. Don Tommaso Silvestrini affirmed: "He told me personal things that were hidden in my very conscience which I had never revealed to anyone." Some people said they were so sure that he could read their thoughts, that every time they had to meet him, they would go to confession first. At Pievetorina he said to the father Superior of the House there, pointing to a parish priest who had been hostile to the Institute: "I am leaving you with a new Missionary." The father Superior was amazed at this. As soon as Gaspar left, that parish priest, who had never dreamt of becoming a missionary or of entering Religious Houses, asked the father Superior to be admitted.

There are also numerous events which show that Gaspar had the gift of *giving wise counsel*. Thus it is not surprising that many came to him for advice and confided in him. A priest told him that he wanted to join the Congregation. Gaspar told him that other things were in store for him. In fact, he became Bishop of Terracina. We already know the story of Don Biagio Valentini. During the Mission at Cori he advised a young man to become a priest, but he did not heed him. Although he was rich, he was reduced to poverty and suffering many adversities in his life, as Gaspar had predicted to him. Don Ferdinando Angelici relates that in 1820 he was studying philosophy and was invited to meet Gaspar who happened to be at Pievetorina. Gaspar, reading into his conscience "had found it somewhat muddled" and invited him to stay on for the Exercises. When he went back to school, he decided to abandon his studies for the priesthood and to become a doctor. At another meeting with Gaspar, the latter clearly told him: "You shall be a doctor of souls and not of bodies." But he stubbornly stuck to his medical studies. One morning, however, he woke up to find he had suddenly had a change of heart and he opted for the priesthood. We already know that Don Innocenzo Betti, who wanted to become a Capuchin, in the end took Gaspar's advice, became a Missionary and was very happy with his choice. He said to Don Filippo Berga, a Basilian monk who wanted to leave the Monastery to help his mother: "You shall be back soon," thus predicting the imminent demise of his mother. To a young pupil who wanted to leave the Institute he said: "If you leave the Institute, you will encounter many sorrows." And so it came to pass. To a young woman who was about to get married he said: "You will become a nun." She, who had no intention of doing any such thing, laughed at the thought. But she ended up not marrying and becoming a nun.

Don Marcellino Brandimarte relates the following: "I had been thinking of leaving the Congregation for some time. I was living in the House at Albano and was trying to keep my thoughts a secret. I noticed, however, that the Servant of God paid particular attention to me and guided me with a most peculiar paternal affection, as though he could see the profound torment that was troubling me. Certain that he knew everything, I revealed my intention to him. He advised me to reflect on the matter. On day, at sunset, he took me in front of the Church of the Capuchins, where a large Cross was standing. He had me admire the beauty of the landscape and then he invited me to kiss the cross. We said a prayer together and then he said: 'You see, my son, I have prayed much. It is God's will that you remain a Missionary.' I saw that his eyes were wet with tears and, in a voice full of sorrow he repeated to me three times: 'You leave a cross of gold and burden yourself with many heavy crosses which you will not be able to bear.' I too, was moved. But I was firm. I left and suffered a host of troubles. I even ended up in prison in the Holy Office."

Don Domenico Silvestri tells the following story about

himself: "When I was a sub–deacon, the Blessed Gaspar told me that I would become a Missionary. Since I suffered from a serious speech impediment, I pointed this out. But he answered that St. Francis Xavier would have interceded and that through his grace I would have been able to preach on Missions. And this all came to pass as he had foretold." To Don Francesco Zanni of Malta who wanted to leave the Institute, he predicted that he would come to a bad end. He did not listen and when he went back to his country he became mad. A young pupil, after a year of being in the ongregation wanted to leave it. Gaspar, in the presence of the boy's father tried to prevent him from doing so, predicting that he would "lead a life full of anguish". They paid him no heed and unfortunately the said prediction came true. He had the infallible gift of being able to distinguish when certain manifestations were the result of illness or diabolic possession.

Gaspar had the gift of *prophecy* and foresaw many future events quite clearly, all of which came to pass in due course, even those in the distant future. He predicted a number of events in his own personal life. We have already mentioned that he had foreseen all the suffering he would undergo. He predicted that he would not reach old age and to his assistant, Bartolomeo, he predicted that he would die after him and after his death he would clothe his lifeless body. He also predicted that he would die after being bled, which in fact occurred. Many of his predictions concerned the future of the Congregation. He predicted well beforehand and in great detail the opening of the Houses at Porto Recanati and in Rome. Valentini recounts that when he was in bed seriously ill, Gaspar, who was by his side led the conversation to Ancona and told him that he, as his successor, would open a House there. In fact, he was the one who opened it in 1839, after Gaspar's death. He predicted great tribulations for the Institute and indeed, it was vehemently opposed, with consequent closing of Houses, suspension of subsidies and suppression and vilification of its Missionaries. Some of his predictions have come to pass as recently as in our own time. But Gaspar has made his personal protection felt. Merlini testified without any possibility of misunderstanding that Gaspar predicted he would become a Missionary and his second successor. He told Sillani, Bishop of Terracina, that he would renounce his post and become a Missionary. Fontana relates that, as he was leaving the House at Frosinone to go to St. Felix, Gaspar handed him some money to buy himself a cloak. He pointed out that he had recently acquired one and would not need the money. But with a smile Gaspar had insisted, saying: "You'll need it, you'll need it." Along the way his cloak was stolen. Can. Moscatelli relates that Gaspar had told him he would be calling on his help to preach at Gaeta and that he would get there by sea from his residence at Terracina. He thought that Gaspar was joking because one normally went quite comfortably from Terracina to Gaeta by land. When he was called, however, along with Bishop Mons. Manasse, he actually made the journey by sea because the usual route had been flooded and was made impassable because of the storms.

Leaving one of the Mission Houses he warned his brothers that under no circumstances were they to go into the kitchen. One of them out of curiosity, disobeyed and found there that the cook was so enraged that he narrowly missed being stabbed in the stomach. Mons. Pellei, Bishop of Acquapendente, relates that it was past noon when he arrived, tired and starved, at Frosinone. Remembering that there were Missionaries there who were his friends, he went there without giving any warning to get something to eat. As soon as he rang the bell, Gaspar himself was at the door to welcome him, as though he had been expecting him. Lunch was already on the table waiting for him. The Bishop tried to leave, thinking that the preparations had been made for someone else. He was surprised indeed when they informed him that lunch had been set for him and that they were not expecting anyone else. We have already mentioned the man at Sermonetta who died immediately after having gone to confession. At the Monastery at Priverno he advised the Prioress to admit a young woman who suffered from extreme convulsions and that she should be given the name of Francesca Saveria because she would soon be completely cured. It came to pass as he had predicted. This young woman later became the Founder of the Perpetual Adorers of the Sacred Heart at Lugo and was regarded as a saint when she died. He predicted that the invalid Don Nicola Maiorano would not die of the serious illness which had brought him to the verge of death. He did in fact recover. Mons. Lucchesi relates that at Spello, Gaspar insisted that the last Sacraments be administered to a sick man whom he did not know, even though his illness was not particularly serious; instead he died the following day. At Veroli, during recreation period, he turned the conversation toward death and asked: "Who among us will be the first to die?" Then he turned toward the two youngest among them, Don Renzi and Don Agostini and told them both to be prepared. Both of them died shortly afterwards, a few months apart. Also at Spello he told Luigi Fortini, who seemed to be in good health, that his death was imminent. He also told another person who had been feeling quite fine at the beginning of the Mission to prepare himself because he would not see the end of it. Both of these predictions came true. He told Mons, Manasse, Bishop of Terracina, that he would die after seven years in office. He told Don Aloisi, whose health was always precarious, that he would die of senile phthisis (consumption). He told Don Antonio Lipparelli that he would live on for another twenty years. He predicted the death of Pius VII, the election and brief reign of Cardinal Della Genga, Leo XII and Pius VIII. He foresaw the sad events of 1848. He also predicted the promotion of some priests to the post of Bishop, among these was Don Gregorio Muccioli. He told Mons. Saverio Siniscalchi that his being bishop would be "like a curse". In fact after only a few years he had to renounce the see at Sanseverino. More than once he told Merlini that he would recover. He told St. Vincenzo Pallotti, who was on the verge of death, that he would recover. He also foresaw the plague which afflicted Rome. At Frosinone, while they were at the table, he turned suddenly to Valentini, urged him to get up immediately and to go to get him a book in the room next door. A few others had got up to go in his stead when he ordered them to stay at their places. Don Valentini had just got up when a flash of lightning struck the place where he had been sitting, burning the chair and the table cloth.

Another gift was that of *bilocation*. At Meldola, as we have already pointed out, while he was preaching in the square, he was seen at the same time sitting in the confessional in the church. This phenomenon took place at Spello also, both during the preaching of a Mission and six years later. A serious rift had arisen among the Brothers of the Oratory. It was determined with certainty that on that day and at that same moment he was preaching in Rome, and yet he was there trying to restore peace.

The gift of ecstasy. We have already mentioned on a number of occasions the episode of ecstasy which Gaspar experienced. We may now say that to be in a state of ecstasy was almost common for him. We know that ever since childhood "he was always in union with God and after Communion his mother had to shake him to bring him back to reality". He was neither playing a role nor was he consciously putting on a show; when he prayed he went into a trance. His periods of ecstasy took place almost always in front of the tabernacle, while he was celebrating Mass or while praying before the Crucifix or the Virgin.

At Montalto they were frantically searching for him because he had not shown up on time for the sermon. They finally found him behind the altar of the Most Holy Sacrament absorbed in prayer. At Pereto, in 1827, the priests who had gathered to listen to his lectures, found him one day floating a hand's breadth above the floor in front of the Tabernacle. In the chapel of the Clarisse at Piperno, one of the sisters came upon him by surprise as he was immobile and radiant before the Tabernacle. When she went to him for confession she innocently asked him how often he went into ecstasy and how long the episodes lasted. He answered: "We must always remain with God." In the Duomo at Todi, after mass was over and everyone had left the church, the sexton passed by shaking his keys before locking up, and saw him in ecstasy, as still as a statue in front of the Tabernacle. He had to shake him because he had not even heard the keys jangling. He was seen on several occasions hovering a few centimetres above the step on the altar while he was celebrating Mass; for example, at Campoli Appennino and at Pievetorina. At Gaeta, while he was preaching in the square, he was seen levitating above the platform. Quite often he was rapt in ecstasy during periods of meditation, and not only at church or at home, but also while he was travelling as many of his Missionaries who saw him have attested. It was not unusual for them to see, both during the day and at night, bright rays of light emanating from the cracks in his door and windows. When they went up to the door and opened it very quietly or if they peeked through the key–hole, they would see him on his knees in front of the Crucifix surrounded by bright light.

THE MIRACLES

Little by little, by mentioning the major places where he performed his missionary work, we have also mentioned a number of extraordinary events; we will give a short summary of them here and ask the reader to excuse the inevitable repetitions.

Merlini narrates a number of prodigious facts the Saint took part in and he prefaces his remarks with: "Along with the angelic Saint Thomas, I will state that a miracle occurs when something happens which is outside the normal course of nature... whence that which is superior to the force of nature appears to be miraculous. It differs from grace in that the latter, according to Benedict XIV, is an example of a particular kind of miracle, due to a specific circumstance of time, place or person. I will therefore relate the facts in the manner in which I came to know them, without adding anything or subtracting anything and with those circumstances which are known to me." We too, shall attempt to emulate Merlini, recounting the facts as Merlini himself transmitted them as well as those from other sources which are very reliable.

Here are some of these:

At Mergo a poor woman who could not move had herself brought to his confessional and asked him to cure her. Gaspar told her to have herself brought before the painting of St. Francis Xavier so that she could pray to him. She was healed before she got there. At Veroli, Antonia Calvani who had for years been suffering from loss of blood and had been declared incurable by her doctors, managed to each him through the crowd and touch the hem of his cassock; she was cured on the spot like the haemorrhaging woman in the Gospel. At Priverno he healed a young woman who had a serious chest ailment. At Ariccia Gaspar was carrying the cross which was to be "erected" in memory of the Mission held there. A woman came up to Merlini

carrying a child who could not walk. Merlini told her to go to Gaspar. The child grasped onto Gaspar's cassock. The next day he was seen running about with the other children. Many years later Merlini saw him again completely cured. At Cori a mother showed him her little "crippled" daughter; Gaspar blessed her and she was healed. At Mergo a man went to visit him and pleaded with him to cure his son who is seriously ill. Gaspar told him that if he donated twelve sacks to the Confraternity of St. Francis Xavier, his son would be cured. As soon as he had delivered the sacks, his son was healed.

In September 1824, he was called by the parish priest Don Felice De Benedictis to the bedside of a youth who was dying. Gaspar sprinkled holy water of St. Francis Xavier on him and he was immediately cured. At Sant'Anatolia, an enraged madman entered the dining rooms where Gaspar and his Missionaries were seated. He gave him a piece of ham which he had blessed and the man was cured. Teresa Cecchini, who was mentally ill, was constantly running away from home, ripping off her clothes and committing other strange acts, was brought before him. He blessed her and thereby cured her on the spot. In 1829 at Macerata Feltria he cured Federico Corradini, who was mentally ill and had become so dangerous because of his condition that he had to be kept chained up in prison. Merlini tells how Gaspar healed a young boy who had injured his knee so badly with a pruning knife that he would never have been able to walk again. Pedini relates how he cured seriously ill people at Giano dell'Umbria. At Albano he cured his faithful servant Bartolomeo of a serious malady which greatly distorted his feet. He cured many sick people at Fiammenga, Sonnino and Sora. Pallotti, aside from his being cured of a mortal illness, relates also of the cure of Abbot Mazzani, of Don Bellini, of Sister Constanza and Paolo Di Pietro. Even the water which the Saint had used to wash himself cured a number of sick people at Spello. Father Barrera dei Dotttrinari writes that at Pontecorvo a pupil of his, who could never remember anything, had perfect

The healing of Francesco Campagna, the first miracle accepted for his canonization.

recall when Gaspar put his hands on his head. With his hand in the act of proffering a blessing, he stopped a farmer whose horse had bolted and prevented him from falling over a cliff. He commanded Don Giambattista Pedini, who had been lying in bed for several months at Frosinone suffering from high fever, to get up and leave immediately for Rome. The sick man obeyed without protest and was immediately cured. Michele De Mattias of Vallecorsa, in 1827, unable to obtain permission to plant tobacco in a piece of land he owned, planted maize instead so as not to lose a growing season.

When the corn had already grown, the permission he had asked for arrived. He talked about it to Gaspar who advised him to destroy the corn and plant tobacco in its stead because he would earn more money. Although the planting had taken place late, the tobacco crop on that land was the best and most abundant of all the farmers in the area. At Giano the community had run out of wine; he blessed the barrel and excellent wine continued to pour from the spout for another 15 days. Another time, still at St. Felix, they were also without wine, while they were dining, they suddenly saw a donkey coming in with two barrels of wine strapped to its back. It so happened that as the animal was passing near the Mission House, it jerked on its lead, got away and passing through the doorway, made its way into the refectory which was on the ground floor. The donkey's owner was quite happy and said: "it must have been God's will that I donate this wine to Father Gaspar." We should also relate the many times that Gaspar's life was spared by divine intervention on occasions when very serious accidents took place, especially hen the horses bolted while he and his Missionaries were being transported by carriage. At Fabriano he remained unharmed by a shower of boiling water which a perverse woman, out of hatred, had poured over him from a window. At Todi a landlord shot at him at point blank range because Gaspar would not tell him what one of his stewards had revealed during confession. The bullet fell harmlessly at his feet. Similarly, there were no ill effects from a drink he ingested at Forlimpopoli in which poison had been poured. Also at Forlimpopoli, according to Valentini, a terrible assassin had been sent from Forlimpopoli to kill him. As soon as he raised the knife to drive it into Gaspar's heart, he felt a mysterious force immobilize his arm and the knife dropped at Gaspar's feet. The hired killer fell to his knees and wept before Gaspar. A Missionary relates: "I was the treasurer at St. Felix and I did not have enough money to pay for the necessary purchases. And we were burdened with debt besides. Our community consisted of twenty individuals and I wrote to Rome about it to the Servant of God. He answered that if I had faith, I would soon see miracles happening. I obeyed and opened the drawer in the presence of the serving brother, Angelo Pontoni, and in the bowl, where previously we were sure there were only five *paoli*, now we found five shining Roman *piastre* with the image of Pius VII on them." At Albano and Frosinone the weight of the wax was found mysteriously to have increased.

At Rimini, they were at the end of a barrel of wine which had become musty. Gaspar blessed it and the wine not only became excellent, but lasted for quite a long time. At Cesena, as Don Angelo Primavera relates, there was a debt of five hundred *scudi* and therefore, he did not want to accept the position of Prior. Gaspar encouraged him to take the post and told him that Providence would help him. Within eleven months and without either asking anyone's help or letting the Community do without, he managed to pay off the debt. "From a human standpoint," Don Primavera concludes, "the fact is in itself unbelievable, and only the holiness of its Founder could have brought about such a miracle." Another Superior attests that he had received three hundred *scudi* from Gaspar, the exact amount he needed. After he had payed expenses, he found he still had a hundred scudi left over. He checked his figures and, thinking Gaspar might have made a mistake, he wrote to him about it. No, he had not made a mistake, he had given him only three hundred, the same amount the missionary had paid out. Gaspar told him: "Let us thank God who sees the purpose for which such expenditures are incurred." Merlini narrates that at Cori the son of Count Giuseppe Cataldi, Francesco, while he was putting a hole in a candle, pierced right through his middle finger with the nail he was using. Gaspar told him to faithfully recite three Hail Marys to the Virgin and urged him to carry the heavy Crucifix. During the Procession the bandage fell from his finger and he saw that the serious wound had totally healed. Again, Merlini relates, as he heard it from Don Francesco Pierantoni, that at Fiammenga, Gaspar gave the parish priest the Relic of St. Francis Xavier so that he might take it and bless a woman with it who was suffering from incurable haemorrhaging and the woman was in fact healed.

"I heard it said," Merlini relates, "that at Ariccia in 1821, a woman was bedridden and unable to move. I remember that on that occasion Gaspar blessed an image of St. Francis Xavier and sent it to the invalid, sending her the message that she should have herself brought to the Mission. She went to it on her own." "At Alatri while he was on a Mission, a boy's foot was healed after washing it with water which Gaspar had blessed." "The Archpriest, Don Luigi Grossi of Lenola, wrote that when Gaspar was there to hold a Mission, he was asked by local farmers as he was leaving, to bless an olive grove that had not borne fruit for many years. After he had blessed it the trees on that site bore fruit but none of the trees in the surrounding groves did so." "While I was at Sermoneta Gaspar called me to him and along the way my leg was bitten by insects and became so swollen that I was scarcely able to get to Albano and, once there, I could not walk. I bathed the leg. Gaspar wanted me to walk but I told him that I was unable to. He disapproved of the baths. I asked him to bless the foot with the Relic of St. Francis Xavier. After the blessing I walked about freely and felt no more discomfort." Again Merlini says: "(Don Biagio Valentini) told me that Don Pasquale Aloisi went to Gaspar and asked to be accepted into the Congregation. However, he was of a certain age and could barely hold remain standing with the help of a cane. Gaspar took one arm and Don Biagio the other and began pacing him about the room. Soon he was standing up without the cane...and then he walked about freely on his own...I seem to remember Gaspar telling me that St. Francis Xavier had performed that miracle."

In a town in Romagna, during the Mission, there was some resentment toward Gaspar because the farmers were expected to attend the sermons. Since it was harvest time, they were afraid that if they didn't pick the grapes when the weather was fine, they risked having some inclement weather ruin the crop. Gaspar assured them that the sermons would not be the cause of any damage to the harvest. Some had faith in the word of the Saint and went to the events. Others had no such trust and even began causing trouble.

The Mission came to an end and then the harvest was completed. The result was that those who had opposed the Mission had a very meagre crop while those who had attended harvested twice as much as they ever had in their best years and the grapes were of the finest quality.

On how many occasions, even though seriously ill had he undertaken very dangerous journeys to preach Missions at which "he found himself miraculously cured". People congratulated him and he answered: "One can never abandon the souls of those who have sinned." Don Beniamino Romani says that he was embarrassed to appear in public because he did not know what to say. Gaspar would put his biretta on Don Romano's head and not only did he no longer have any difficulty preaching, but his sermons had a very great effect. Don Aloisi tells a curious tale which has to do with Gaspar's biretta. Don Aloisi could not overcome the difficulty he had speaking in public either, so Gaspar gave him his biretta as a present and with it on his head, everything worked well. On one occasion, however, he made a mistake and put on his own biretta before climbing onto the platform. He couldn't utter a word. He sent someone to the sacristy to get Gaspar's. When he put it on his head "the words flowed on their own". Other Missionaries as well have said that while wearing the biretta, the sash or the crucifix of Gaspar, they experienced no difficulty in preaching.

He was very caring towards his brothers and it seemed that his magical hand was always available to them. We add a few more episodes on this subject to those already narrated. Don Beniamino Romani relates that Gaspar asked him to go and conduct a Mission at Civitavecchia. He pointed out that a few days earlier he had bled profusely from the chest and that he felt quite ill. Gaspar put his sash around him and placed his own Crucifix on his breast. Not only was he able to take part in the entire Mission in fine form and without ill effects, but he also went, always at his behest, to preach for the month of May at Vallecorsa. Don Giovanni Merlini was called to Poggio Mirteto, where Gaspar was holding a Mission. Since he had no other means of transportation available, he was forced to make the journey on foot and at night, and arrived to Poggio with such a high fever that he lapsed into unconsciousness several times. He spent the night in bed, but very early next morning Gaspar came into his room and said with a smile: "Don Giovanni, it is time for the sermon. Please wake up..." Merlini got up immediately and as soon as he began preaching he felt fine and took up all the normal duties of a Mission, preaching, confessing and the other functions. We also know that Merlini, who was very hard of hearing, through the intercession of Gaspar's prayers was able to hear during confessions and during spiritual conversations.

One day at Albano after lunch, while the Missionaries were at recreation, he was brought the news that Don Fontana was dying. He told the brothers and added: "Let us go to pray to the Virgin for him," and they all gathered in the church. After a few days they learned that the dying man had begun to get better at that exact same hour and subsequently recovered completely. Don Angelo Primavera was also cured of a serious malady to his stomach after eating some food which Gaspar had blessed. It often happened that some of the Missionaries who became gravely ill, especially while preaching alongside him, would be cured by him and were thus enabled to continue with the Mission.

Unfortunately, divine retribution was not lacking against those who were opposed to his ministry or who tried to harm him. A number of Sectarians at Forlimpopoli had set out to kill him. Once they were facing him, they became so frightened that in running away their carriage overturned and they all died. As soon as he learned the news he said: "May God have mercy on those unfortunate souls," and he went off to pray. A certain man from Bastiano di Penne who had uttered much slander against Gaspar died of cancer of the tongue, even though he was very young. Even the odd priest who opposed his ministry and wrote letters full of calumny against him from Romagna to Rome, was clearly punished by Divine Justice.

Are these (of which we have spoken) the only great gifts with which God enriched his chosen Servant and the only miracles which he performed through the grace of the Blood of Christ?

We think not. He was extremely humble and tried to hide these talents since he felt himself to be a great sinner and unworthy of them. He shunned praise from his fellow man and would always sincerely point out his own defects. God exalted him also because of this humility, for he raises up the humble and strikes down the haughty in spirit.

Now we shall narrate those miracles which the Church examined with scrupulous care and scientific rigour and which served to confer upon him the honour of being venerated at the Altar.

IN THE GLORY OF HEAVEN
AND ON THE THRONE OF THE ALTAR

Since we have had to be brief in our narration, we have rightly limited ourselves to a few remarks on the illustrious and heroic virtues of the Saint, to his supernatural gifts, to the prodigious events and miracles performed by him during his life and after his death.

The reputation he enjoyed as a Saint while alive grew enormously after his death. Indeed, it became so widespread that it crossed the borders of Italy and Europe, thus multiplying the number of those – common people, cardinals, bishops, officials and important personages – who were desirous of seeing him officially and solemnly recognized by the Church by elevating him to the status of Sainthood.

We know that the Church, and rightly so, allow many years to pass before passing judgement and requires that miracles be proved before canonization can take place. First it examines rigorously the heroic nature of the virtues by going through the documents and the sworn testimony. Then, with equal rigour, using the expertise of a medical committee and other controls of the Congregation of the Saints, it evaluates the miracles attributed to the Servants of God. In the time of the Venerable Gaspar, four miracles were required, two for the Beatification and, after the Beatification, two for the canonization.

On March 19, 1891, Pope Leo XIII issued the Decree through which he recognized that the Venerable Don Gaspar Del Bufalo had possessed all of the virtues of a heroic nature.

Pius X solemnly decreed his Beatification on August 29, 1904, after having approved the two required miracles on May 29. On December 18, 1904 he proceeded with great solemnity to beatify him in the Vatican Basilica. We now relate the two miracles.

The first occurred to the shepherd Ottavio Lo Stocco of Lenola (in the province of Latina) in 1838, just a year after the Saint's death. From childhood Ottavio had been afflicted with a variety of diseases and had thus grown up to be very delicate and his health was always in a precarious state, especially his chest. His work as a shepherd, which exposed him to the elements and other hardships, also contributed to his ill–health, so much so that the sickness in his lungs had brought him very close to dying. He was seen by the best doctors, among whom was Prof. Notarianni, one of the most famous specialists of that time, whose opinion was that the tuberculosis, along with other complications, had reached such a stage that it was beyond the scope of medical science to give any hope. It was the parish priest who, when he saw him vomiting little bits of lung, suggested placing his faith and hope in the hands of the Venerable Don Gaspar Del Bufalo. When the family had gathered together, he gave him the Relic of the Venerable Man to swallow. Already during that night, an extraordinary thing happened which had not occurred for a long time: his coughing ceased and he slept peacefully and without interruption. The next day he got out of bed and his doctor, who had been called in to examine him, to his great amazement, found the patient to be in good health.

No less amazing is the second miracle which took place at Albano Laziale to Clementina Masini in 1861. The poor woman was suffering from "chronic exudative peritonitis, which then became acute and followed by purulence of the peritoneum, taking on the form of a cyst, with perforations of the abdominal surface and the underlying intestine". The disease got worse each day without any of the "luminaries of medicine" being able to do anything except to say that a cure was impossible. Since a great stench emanated from her, she was abandoned by her husband and family. In despair as to what to do she had herself transported to the Church of the Venerable Don Gaspar Del

Bufalo and had herself lowered onto his tomb. She found such relief lying in that position that she would have preferred never to leave. We should point out that in bed, in that same position, the pain would not cease. Day and night she prayed for the help of the Venerable Gaspar. She swallowed his relic, and finally, on the night of January 21, 1861, the Servant of God appeared to her in the garb of a Missionary and as she desperately called to him, he touched the infected area with his staff saying to her: "Come, woman. Do not be afraid. Tomorrow morning you will get up and will no longer be ill." On hearing those words, she trustingly fell asleep. The next morning she awoke completely cured.

Another 50 years went by. A great man, Pope Pious XII, himself a Saint, also born in Rome like St. Gaspar and a great devotee of his, was to proclaim him a Saint. On the evening of June 12, 1954, after having approved the required two miracles in May of the same year, the proclamation took place during the pontifical celebration in St. Peter's square.

In the years between his Beatification and his Canonization, the Congregation of St. Gaspar, overcoming with the help of God and the Saint great trials and the shock of the Second World War, and suffering great damage to its Houses, had spread out to the whole world and had founded Foreign Missions, thus giving proof of the continuous protection of its Founder.

Almost as a prelude to the Canonization of the Saint came the Beautification of the Venerable Maria De Mattias, founder of the Adoring Sisters of the Blood of Christ, decreed by Pius XII on July 22, of the Holy Year 1959 and solemnly proclaimed at St. Peter's the following October.

The first miracle approved for his Canonization happened to Francesco Campagna at Campoli Appennino, where the Blessed Gaspar was greatly venerated and his feast day was celebrated every year. As we know, he had been there many times to preach during his lifetime and he had performed prodigious feats there. The young man had been in bed for some time suffering from bronchial pneumonia and acute meningitis. The doctor's had predicted that his death was imminent. He was only twenty years old and one can imagine the feeling of despair that gripped him and his family. On May 19, 1929 the statue of the Blessed

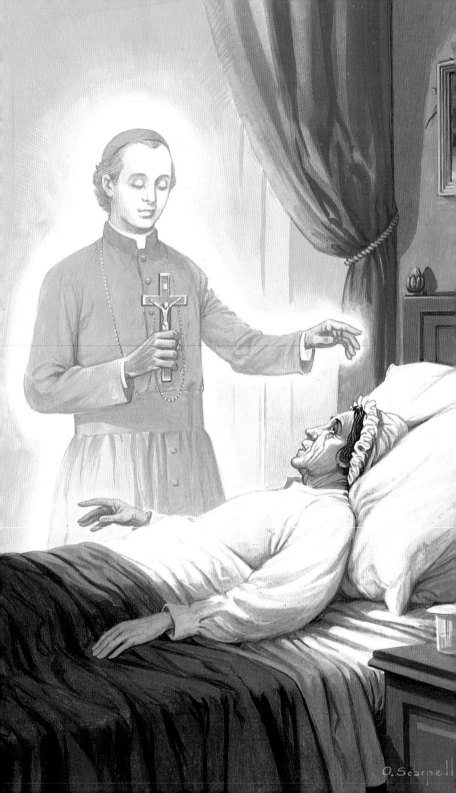

O. Scarpelli

Gaspar was being carried in the procession and it passed by right below the balcony of the room where the sick youth lay. Upon hearing the singing of the faithful, he freed himself from his relatives, who on seeing him so agitated had tried to restrain him thinking he might injure himself, rushed towards the balcony and throwing himself on his knees began to shout: "Grant me grace, grant me grace, Blessed Gaspar." The crowd picked up his cry: Grace, Grace, Blessed Gaspar!" After the procession had gone by, he was taken back to the bed where he fell into a deep, long sleep from which he awoke completely cured.

The second miracle occurred at Sezze Romano, to the widow, Orsola Bono. She was the mother of two Sisters of the Adorers of the Blood of Christ, a priest, Don Francesco Pontecorvi and of another son, Ciro, who was a pupil of the Missionaries of St. Gaspar. Her brother–in–law, Don Ciro Pontecorvi was a Missionary of the Most Precious Blood and Archbishop of Urbino. She was afflicted with a malignant tumour in the abdomen. At the then Hospital of the Littorio in Rome, the chief surgeon refused to operate on her given the advanced state of the malady and he "sent her home to die". Her children gave her a Relic of the Blessed Gaspar to swallow and along with the sick woman began to pray to him with faith and hope. She was unable to retain even liquids and was almost totally paralyzed. During the night, when the illness had reached its pinnacle, she saw the figure of a priest at the foot of her bed. Thinking it was her son Don Francesco, she called out to him to tell him that she felt very ill. Instead it was the Blessed Gaspar who spoke to her: "I am not Don Francesco, but the Blessed Gaspar. Take heart, soon you will be well." And so it came to pass, for in the morning, to the amazement of all those who were present, she got out of the bed completely cured.

Many people, on hearing so many wonders told, remain sceptical and seek to find in the mysterious forces of nature an explanation for them. But those who have faith, bow their heads and exalt the power of God, creator of all things who is able to

The healing of Orsola Bono, the second miracle approved for his canonization.

change even the course of nature herself, so that mankind may benefit from it and His Saints may be praised.

HIS MESSAGE

Reading a biography or saying a prayer is not enough if one wishes to become a true disciple of a saint. One must also understand and receive his message.

All saints, before becoming our protectors, were first teachers of mankind. There are the renowned Doctors of the Church, the saints of charity, the great apostles. Through their heroic virtues, their actions and their words, each of them has passed on his message.

What is the message of St. Gaspar?

He was a saint of many talents, but his distinctive symbol was the Blood of Christ, that is the greatest sacrifice that God in his boundless love has ever given us. With the reading of his brief history, then, there should remain with us the image of a saint who worked and suffered in the name of the Divine Blood and for the Divine Blood of Christ. By virtue of that Blood, he developed his profound commitment to the life of the spirit and his zeal for the salvation of souls. Through sheer strength of will he endured unbearable suffering and adversity in order to become more like the Crucified Christ. He flooded his soul with that Blood which cries out to us with divine love, and he burned with the desire to sacrifice in turn his own blood for his Lord. In a groan of unappeased desire he laments: "I have not yet loved Christ to the last drop of my blood."

He understood the value of each soul redeemed at the cost of all of the Blood of Jesus and he in turn burned with the desire to bring to Him all those souls whom sin had caused to stray. Through words and deeds, through love and commitment of all his energy on behalf of the poor, the persecuted, those on the fringe of society, the sinners in whom he saw the suffering Christ personified he served humanity. He did not run, he flew from town to town, through the streets, the valleys, the mountains, the hide outs of the brigands, and into the prisons to bring the word of Christ, his love, his forgiveness. No illness, no difficulty, no wilful opposition, no obstacle could stop him, right up to the end of his earthly existence. "Sitio! I am thirsty!" The same cry issued from his lips that Christ uttered on the cross for the salvation of souls.

Gaspar has shown us what power of salvation can reside in the soul, and how explosive the action of one man can be if he truly loves God, and only God, above all other things.

And so the voice of Gaspar has not been extinguished, nor will it ever remain silent. Especially if we fellow missionaries, and then all those who are devoted to him, first learn to make his message their own, and then transmit it from generation to generation.

The Saints, before being called upon for help, should first of all be imitated to the best of our ability.

St. Gaspar, next to Peter and Paul the greatest apostle of the Blood of Christ, will guide us in the spirituality of that Blood, will continue always to speak to us of that Blood, will help us to pursue and enjoy the glory of that Blood.

INDEX